She Speaks

She Speaks

WISDOM FROM THE WOMEN *of the*
BIBLE *to the* MODERN BLACK WOMAN

MICHELE CLARK JENKINS

Sisters in FAITH

THOMAS NELSON
Since 1798

NASHVILLE   DALLAS   MEXICO CITY   RIO DE JANEIRO

Published in Nashville, Tennessee, by Thomas Nelson. Thomas Nelson is a registered trademark of Thomas Nelson, Inc.

Images: istock.com, vectorstock.com

Thomas Nelson, Inc., titles may be purchased in bulk for educational, business, fund-raising, or sales promotional use. For information, please e-mail SpecialMarkets@ThomasNelson.com.

Unless otherwise noted, Scripture quotations are taken from the KING JAMES VERSION.

ISBN: 978-1-4016-7780-0

Printed in the United States of America

12 13 14 15 16 RRD 6 5 4 3 2 1

Contents

Letter

Hello, our sister,

We, Stephanie and Michele, met on a Bible project many years ago. Since then we have been real sisters in faith. We have seen each other through the ups and downs of our lives, shared our dreams and our desires, worked together, played together, wondered what God had in store for us together, and sometimes had disagreements. But Christ has always been at the center of our relationship as we each make choices that take us closer to Him and make us more like Him.

The *Sisters in Faith* brand is an extension of our relationship. We want to see all of our sisters reach out to one another and their families to establish Christ-centered relationships, to develop their own self-worth through the eyes of a God that loves them, to strive for God purposed careers; and most of all to develop a closer walk with Jesus.

Sisters in Faith was created to provide tools to encourage and empower African American women in God's Word, but we also invite all women to hear our hearts. *She Speaks* is one of those tools; it is designed to demonstrate how inclusive God's Word is. The women who are presented in the Old and New Testaments are not there by accident, nor are they there just to be wallpaper to the men in the Bible. If you read their stories, you will quickly see that God loved them, He spoke to them, He called them, He taught them, He used them, He honored them, He blessed them, and He demonstrated many Kingdom principles through their lives. We hope that the message of their lives encourages and empowers you!

May the Lord bless you!

—Michele Clarke Jenkins & Stephanie Perry Moore
Sisters in Faith General Editors

Acknowledgments

Thank you, Jesus! I am so grateful for the desire You have planted in my heart and the opportunity to write You have provided. I only want to do your will and make You known to as many people as I can.

Thank you, Thomas Nelson, for wanting to present the hearts of African American, Christian women and to reach our communities; specifically, I want to thank Heather McMurray and Alee Anderson for catching the vision right away and saying yes to almost everything Stephanie and I wanted to do; and Bob Sanford, you will always be my friend and mentor. Gary Davidson, a good work that you began will continue to be to your credit. Brenda Noel and Dawn Sherrill of Echo Creative Media, thank you for being the best editors and friends a writer could have. To Keren Heath, for your excerpts from the *Place of Honor* feature from the *Sisters in Faith Devotional Bible*, I send my appreciation. To my partner, Stephanie, you are in this with me, and we have so much more to do for God's Kingdom. I can't wait to see what He has for us next.

To my big sisters: Judy Clark, Karen Clark, and Marcia McEntyre, I send real love for introducing me to the concept of sisterhood. No matter how far away we are from each other, or how long it has been since we've seen each other, we have a shared family experience that snaps right back whenever we are together. Thank you to my own girls: Winnie, Abi, and Kymi, for singing that silly song you made up, "Sisters, Sisters, we are Sisters" as you swayed together, arms around each other and giggling. It lets me know that you will stay close no matter what. Thank you to my husband, Kym Jenkins, for protecting my time so I could write these pages.

I also want to note that my oldest daughter, Winnie, designed the beautiful pages of this book. Kate Mulvaney, the Art Director on this project, worked hard to bring this cover to what it is. My thanks to them all.

Introduction

The fifty women presented in *She Speaks* all lived in very different times and places than where we, as modern women, dwell. But every one of their lives can be a beacon to our own, in this modern day, through God's timeless Word. Their stories begin in a first person telling, so they can personalize their lives for you. The remaining format will help you understand where and why they were placed in God's Word. I have even highlighted the women from our own heritage, so you will see that women who looked like us were part of God's plan.

Following each story are the references to these women in the King James Version of the Bible. I encourage you to always let what I write lead you to read God's Word for yourself. Even though I've tried to tell their stories in a convenient format, nobody can tell it better than God!

If you will, when you've finished reading each story and scripture, ask God to show you what He has for you to learn from that woman's life. I am praying that His revelations to you are life changing.

I will continue to keep you in my prayers, my sister. Please keep me in yours.

Blessings & Honor,

Michele Clark Jenkins

I AM

Eve

*And the rib, which the Lord
God had taken from man,
made he a woman, and
brought her unto the man.*

Genesis 2:22

I was the first woman. I was in that beautiful garden named Eden and I was not alone. I had Adam, to whom I was a helpmate, and I had God. God was my Father and He was good to me and provided for all of my needs.

However, I just didn't understand why God told Adam He didn't want us to taste the fruit from the Tree of the Knowledge of Good and Evil. I grew more and more curious. Then we got company. It was a snake; and it spoke to me questions that sounded much like my own. But he took it even further, saying God just didn't want Adam and me to rise to His level. He told me that if we ate from the tree, we would be as God. He told us we would not die if we ate the forbidden fruit, although God told us that we would.

I chose to believe the serpent. I didn't want to get in trouble with God, at least not by myself, so I talked Adam into tasting of the fruit of the tree with me. As we did, terrible things happened. We saw everything around us through our altered, sinful eyes and no longer through the pure, unblemished vision we had known through our unbroken relationship with God. We knew we were in big trouble! So we tried to run from God (which was futile since He is everywhere).

Of course, God found us. The first thing Adam did was tell God I gave him the fruit to eat. What a tattletale! So I explained to God it was really the serpent's fault because he is the one who tricked me. God held Adam and me accountable for our actions and He cast us out of the garden, never to return.

Why Her?

We all remember that Eve broke the only commandment God had given to her through Adam—she believed Satan's lies and ate from the only forbidden tree in the Garden of Eden. And she convinced Adam to do the same. As a result, she also became the agent through whom death entered the world. Wow, talk about your reputation preceding you! She had a lot to live down. It would seem that nothing good could ever have come from Eve. But her sin is not the only thing we remember about Eve; from her we also learn that God can use the worst in us for good.

Eve's name means "source of life." Even though Eve is considered the source of death, as the mother of all living people, God allowed Eve to maintain her purpose as the mother of all life through her son, Seth. It was Seth's children who began to call on the name of the Lord. His children's children waited for the Messiah, one of Eve's own bloodline, to restore true life to all. What an honor God bestowed on this first of sinners.

Eve's name means "source of life."

About Her

Eve was made from the rib of Adam and was the first woman. Before they were driven out, Eve lived with Adam in the Garden of Eden. Among her sons were Cain, Abel, and Seth. She is the mother of all mankind and is responsible, along with Adam, for the first sin that separated us from God.

Apply Her

Eve's sin was that she reasoned and freely chose to be disobedient to what God said. Actually, at the point she made her decision, she didn't care what God said; she cared only for what she wanted. It was her selfishness and self-rule that separated Eve from God, but not from His love.

It is the same with us. We can either choose to accept Jesus as our Lord and Savior, submit to His will, and spend all eternity with Him; or we can choose our own way without Him, which is the path of sin and eternal death.

Find Her

Genesis 1:26–29

Genesis 2:15–25

Genesis 3:1–24

Genesis 4:1, 2, 25, 26

2 Corinthians 11:3

1 Timothy 2:14

I AM Sarah

And God said, Sarah thy wife shall bear thee a son indeed; and thou shalt call his name Isaac: and I will establish my covenant with him for an everlasting covenant, and with his seed after him.

Genesis 17:19

I had prayed and prayed, but the Lord had not seen fit to let me have children. When it seemed God was never going to answer my prayers, I arranged for my husband, Abraham, to be with my handmaiden. That way, he could have a son to continue his line.

Then God showed up. When I was old and worn out, I overheard him telling Abraham that I would give birth within a year. In my head, I was thinking, "What a joke." I'd already been through menopause!

Unfortunately, I laughed out loud and God asked Abraham why I laughed. Then I lied and told God that I hadn't. But God had heard and said, "You did laugh".

As badly as I feel about lying to Him, I am highly honored that He spoke to me and cared about what I thought. I've never heard much about God speaking to any women; but the God of the universe told me He would go against the natural and would supernaturally bless us with a son, Isaac—the answer to my lifelong prayers.

I am a living testimony that, even when the earth treats women like second class citizens, God will answer our prayers. He is faithful even when we've given up asking.

Why Her?

Sarah, wife of Abraham, is considered one of the great women of faith in the Bible; but she also demonstrated a lack of faith when she got tired of waiting on God.

God had promised Abraham, "Look now toward heaven, and tell the stars, if thou be able to number them: and he said unto him, So shall thy seed be" (Gen. 15:5). Yet, Sarah looked at all of her circumstances and determined that she could not be used in God's plan to multiply Abraham's seed. So, she gave another woman, Hagar, her Egyptian maid, to her husband as his wife so he could fulfill God's plan without her. After Hagar gave birth, Sarah saw that this might not have been such a good plan.

Jealousy and competition created some serious drama between Sarah and her ex-handmaiden.

Jealousy and competition created some serious drama between Sarah and her ex-handmaiden. Through all the problems, Sarah still laughed to herself at the thought that God could open up her her ninety-year-old womb to have children. She soon found that nothing is too great for God—Isaac was born to her in her old age. The strife was even greater once Isaac was born. Isaac was God's chosen vessel to carry on the lineage of Abraham; Hagar and

Ishmael were soon forced to leave the camp and begin life in a new country.

All the drama in Sarah's life with Hagar and the issues between their sons, Ishmael and Isaac, could have been avoided if Sarah had just waited for the Lord to do what He promised in His time and in His way.

About Her

Sarai (whose name God changed to Sarah as a symbol of His covenant with her, promising that He would covenant with her child) was both Abraham's wife and his half-sister—they had the same father, Terah, but different mothers. She is also the mother of Isaac and an ancestor in the lineage of Jesus Christ.

Apply Her

Sometimes God whispers in our ears and mobilizes us to take action on His behalf to carry out His will. But Sarah had no such directive from God in choosing to give Hagar to Abraham. God doesn't need our help to move things along or to make things happen. Unless we hear from Him, we should remove our hands from manipulating the lives of others; even if we're doing what we think is best for them. In fact, we could be interfering with God's plans for that person's life and our own.

Find Her

I AM

Hagar

And Sarai said unto Abram, Behold now, the Lord hath restrained me from bearing: I pray thee, go in unto my maid; it may be that I may obtain children by her. And Abram hearkened to the voice of Sarai.

Genesis 16:2

I had a hard life . . . very hard. I was born an Egyptian handmaid and was in service to Abraham's wife, Sarah. When Sarah couldn't get pregnant, she went to her husband and asked if he would have a child with me that Sarah could count her own. So, Sarah gave me to Abraham to be his wife. But when I got pregnant by Abraham, I really just couldn't stand Sarah. I mean, she had it all, and then she wanted to count my son as her own? It was too much to bear; so I just ran away.

I really didn't have anywhere to go; but when I stopped to rest, the angel of God came to me and told me to go back to Sarah and serve her. He promised my son would have a whole nation. What a sacrifice I was asked to make for God! But I didn't hesitate. The God of Abraham was a powerful God, and I believed in Him.

So I went back and had my baby, whom the Lord called Ishmael. Then, wouldn't you know it, eventually, Sarah popped up pregnant as old as she was! Unbelievable! I had not treated Sarah with respect or kindness. And she finally had a son of her own, Isaac. So, of course she didn't want my son anymore and banished both of us from Abraham's camp.

So there we were, out in the wilderness, just my baby and me. I cried because we were out of water. I had trusted God to do what He said, yet there we were, in the middle of nowhere, out of food and water and energy.

But God was faithful and rescued us. I found Ishmael a wife, and he became the father of his own nation with twelve tribes. As for me, I was able to live out my days as a free and blessed woman.

Why Her?

Sarah (Sarai), being unable to have children of her own, gave Hagar, her Egyptian handmaid, to Abraham. Sarah hoped the slave might conceive a child on her behalf. Hagar did conceive a child, but decided to run away because of Sarah's mistreatment.

Pregnant and alone in the middle of the desert, Hagar was comforted when the Angel of the Lord met her and told her to return to Sarah. He promised that, through her son, a great nation would be established. Hagar returned to Sarah with a renewed sense of purpose.

Hagar gave birth to Ishmael (whose name means "God hears"). However, though Ishmael was Abraham's first-born son, he and his mother were expelled from the tribe. Hagar found herself alone once again, but God heard her cry for help and delivered her.

God blessed Hagar and kept His word. Hagar showed great courage and endurance. Once a slave in a foreign nation, she ended her life as a free woman, with a promise from God. (See Gen. 16:1–16; 21:6–21.)

Pregnant and alone in the middle of the desert, Hagar was comforted when the Angel of the Lord met her.

About Her

Hagar was Sarah's handmaiden and the mother of Abraham's son, Ishmael.

Apply Her

God never promised our lives would be free of trials and tribulations. To the contrary, Jesus told us that, as Christians, we would face hard times. But that's not the end of the story. Jesus said, "These things I have spoken unto you, that in me ye might have peace. In the world ye shall have tribulation: but be of good cheer; I have overcome the world" (John 16:33). This means that no matter how badly you start and no matter how long the trouble lasts, God will deliver you from it for His glory and for your good.

Find Her

Genesis 16:1–16

Genesis 21: 9–21

Genesis 25:12–13

I AM
Rebekah

And the children struggled together
within her; and she said, If it be
so, why am I thus? And she went
to enquire of the Lord. And the
Lord said unto her, Two nations are
in thy womb, and two manner of
people shall be separated from thy
bowels; and the one people shall be
stronger than the other people; and
the elder shall serve the younger.

Genesis 25:22–23

hen I was young and beautiful, things just happened for me. I was an obedient young girl who followed God's ways. But even I could not have imagined that one day the servant of Isaac, a rich man, would choose me to become his master's wife.

Isaac was a good husband and he loved me. Everything was perfect until I became pregnant with twin boys. I wondered what I had done to bring curses upon myself; my sons were polar opposites. They fought even in the womb! So I went to the Lord and asked Him what it was all about. He told me my older son, Esau, was to serve my younger son, Jacob. From that point forward, I favored Jacob, but my husband favored Esau.

I know there are many who think I was a manipulative mother; but when I saw my husband planned to give Esau the blessing that the Lord told me was for Jacob, I tried to keep my husband from going against the will of God.

If my life can teach one thing, it's that God will always bring about His own will.

Why Her?

Prayer is dominant in the story of Rebekah. Abraham prayed for a wife for Isaac, and God answered his prayer with Rebekah. Abraham's servant, who was sent to find a wife for Isaac, prayed that God would show him the woman who was to be Isaac's wife; and God answered his prayer by showing Rebekah to him.

When Rebekah had been barren for twenty years, Isaac prayed for her and his prayer was answered—Rebekah gave birth to twin boys. Rebekah prayed to God about her sons. And God showed her that the older son, Esau, would serve the younger son, Jacob. It was because of God's response to her prayer that she favored Jacob and wanted to make sure he received the first-born blessing.

Without prayer, Rebekah's life could have been insignificant and purposeless; instead, she is remembered in the genealogy of Jesus Christ. Like Rebekah, we have to seek God's will through prayer and then conform our lives to the answers He gives.

Abraham prayed for a wife for Isaac and God answered his prayer with Rebekah.

About Her

Rebekah was the daughter of Bethuel, who was the son of Nabor, Abraham's brother. She was married to Isaac, son of Abraham. She was mother to Jacob and Esau. Jacob's name was later changed to Israel by God; it is through him that all the tribes of Israel descend. Jacob is in the lineage of Jesus Christ.

Apply Her

The purposes for each of our lives have already been defined by God. It is up to us to surrender ourselves to His magnificent will so that we will live out the purpose for which we were created. One of the most powerful tools for this accomplishment is prayer. Without prayer, we may miss God's direction and His voice in our lives.

Find Her

Genesis 24:1–67

Genesis 25:20–28

Genesis 26:7–11

Genesis 27:5–46

Genesis 28:5

Genesis 29:12

Genesis 49:30–31

I AM
Rachel

And when Rachel saw that she bare Jacob no children, Rachel envied her sister; and said unto Jacob, Give me children, or else I die.

Genesis 30:1

ith Jacob and me, it was love at first sight. He always intended to marry me and worked seven years for my father in order to earn my hand in marriage. But at the wedding, my father substituted my older sister, Leah, for me because she was the oldest and had to marry first. Poor Jacob had been deceived and had to work another seven years to finally have my hand in marriage.

But then came many years of barrenness for me while my sister presented him with four sons. So, I enlisted my handmaiden, Bilhah, to be my surrogate and she bore him two sons. A kind of battle-of-the-children ensued; Jacob's other wives and consorts gave birth to eleven of Jacob's children. I finally conceived and gave birth to Joseph. Still, there was a competition between my sister and me, and I was not content.

Ironically, I died at an early age giving birth to my second son, Benjamin. My competitive discontentment caused me to have trouble in my marriage and may have ultimately cost me my life.

Why Her?

Rachel was eaten up with jealousy because she was barren while her sister was having children with Jacob. Rachel couldn't rest and felt she had to make things happen—not only because she purely desired children but also because Leah was having children, and she needed to do her sister one better. Giving Bilhah to Jacob so that she could be the surrogate for Rachel's child was wrong on so many levels that it was obviously not of God. But Rachel didn't care what God wanted; this was about what Rachel wanted. In her envy of Leah, she even told Jacob that if she didn't have a child, she would die. How ironic that she died giving birth.

We will never know, on this side of heaven, what the hand of God might have done in Rachel's life. Rachel's hand took control as she tried to model her life after her sister's example and not to God's purpose.

About Her

Rachel was the wife of Jacob and the daughter of Laban. She had an older sister, Leah. Rachel was the mother of both Joseph and Benjamin; and through them were birthed three[1] of the twelve tribes of Israel.

---

1 Joseph's sons, Manesseh and Ephraim were fathers of two of the tribes of Israel.

Apply Her

We have to have patience while we wait on the Lord. If we try to make things happen in our time instead of God's, nothing will be done right, and we might miss God's blessing—on our lives and for generations to come. We cannot look at someone else's life from the outside and claim it as our own. It is foolhardy to think that, just because someone else's life looks perfect to us, they are not facing many struggles. How many rich and famous people have we heard about who literally kill themselves because their lives are so miserably empty?

Competing in life is never of God. What He ordains for us will belong to us. He can offer us a life of our own that will never be empty again. All we have to do is claim it.

Find Her

Genesis 29:6–35

Genesis 30:1–25

Genesis 31: 3–4, 14–34

Genesis 33:1–7

Genesis 35:16–26

Genesis 46:19–25

Genesis 48:7

Ruth 4:11

Matthew 2:18

I AM

Tamar

And Judah acknowledged them,
and said, She hath been more
righteous than I; because that I
gave her not to Shelah my son.
And he knew her again no more.

Genesis 38:26

*S*ometimes, a sister's got to do for herself. You see, God killed my husband, Er, for being wicked. I was left childless. So, as required by God's Law, Er's brother, Onan, took me as wife in order to provide an heir for Er.

Onan married me, but when he slept with me, he spilled his seed on the ground. He knew if I conceived a son, he would be considered Er's descendant. God doesn't like ugly, so he slew Onan. That left Er's brother, Shelah, who was a young boy. So, I waited for my father-in-law, Judah, to bring Shelah to me when he grew into a man, but Judah did not.

So, I took matters into my own hands and tricked Judah into believing I was a prostitute by dressing the part. He hired me and gave me his signet ring, staff, and bracelet as guarantee of payment. He slept with me, and I conceived.

When my pregnancy was discovered, he had the nerve to call me a whore. He didn't know he was the father. Well, I fixed him when I returned his belongings. What could he say? I had only claimed my right to have a child from my husband's lineage. As it turned out, I had twins, one of whom was an ancestor of King David.

This goes to show that God, in His grace, can bring good from even the most messed up situations.

Why Her?

Judah failed to apply God's judgment of Er to his own way-ward lifestyle. He had forgotten the importance of honoring God's Law and had begun to go his own way. After Judah's first son, Er, and his second son, Onan, died after marriage to Tamar, Judah refused to allow his third son, Shelah, to wed her. He did not care it was required by God's Law that he do so. This was a demonstration of Judah's self-rule and rebellion against God.

God not only used Tamar to force Judah to face his sin, but also to confront the hypocritical judgments he had made. Not only did God use this situation to convict Judah of his sin, He also perfected His will through the life of Pharez, one of Tamar's sons.

About Her

Tamar was married to Er and Onan, the sons of Judah, who was the oldest son of Jacob. Tamar was the mother of

God not only used Tamar to force Judah to face his sin, but also to confront the hypocritical judgments he had made.

twins, Pharez and Zarah, whom she conceived by Judah. Pharez was an ancestor of David and is in the lineage of Jesus Christ.

Apply Her

The effect of sin is always the same—it strikes where we are vulnerable and seeks to destroy our lives. Yet No matter how deep the mess, God has promised to use it all for good. (See Rom. 8:28.)

Find Her

Genesis 38:6–30

Ruth 4:12

1 Chronicles 2:4

Matthew 1:1-3

I AM
Asenath

And Pharaoh called Joseph's name Zaphnathpaaneah; and he gave him to wife Asenath the daughter of Potipherah priest of On. And Joseph went out over all the land of Egypt.

Genesis 41:45

Pharaoh gave me to one of his officials, Joseph, to be his wife. I was Egyptian and he was Hebrew. Joseph could not marry me because I was not Hebrew, so I converted.[1] That was important for me to do so that our descendants would be acceptable within the tribes of Israel. When I first married Joseph, Egypt was a land of plenty; but Joseph had cautioned Pharaoh that seven years of famine would come upon Egypt. Joseph was put in charge of storing up food for that time. Before the famine came, Joseph and I had two children, Manasseh and Ephraim.

As Joseph predicted, the famine came and he was a big hero to Pharaoh and the people of Egypt because he stored up enough food so that they would not go hungry. No matter what praise Joseph got from Pharaoh and the Egyptian people, he still missed his family. I was very happy when Joseph found his brothers and his father.

I'm glad I converted to Joseph's faith because our successful union produced two sons, Manasseh and Ephraim. I am proud to say, they each became a father of one of the twelve tribes of Israel.

1   (*Joseph and Asenath*).

Why Her?

Joseph, a Hebrew prisoner of Egypt, was released from prison when he correctly interpreted Pharaoh's dreams about a coming famine. Pharaoh gave Joseph control over all of Egypt, second only to Pharaoh himself. Because Joseph was a Hebrew, he had to be given a new Egyptian name; Pharaoh gave him the name Zaphnathpaaneah. And, in order to connect Joseph to a prominent Egyptian family, Pharaoh gave Asenath to him as a wife. Talk about a power couple!

Asenath bore Joseph two sons; the first he named Manasseh, saying, "For God, said he, hath made me forget all my toil, and all my father's house" (Gen. 41:51). He named his second son Ephraim, saying, "For God hath caused me to be fruitful in the land of my affliction" (Gen. 41:52).

Although the Bible does not tell much about Asenath, we know she fulfilled her destiny as wife and mother

Asenath bore Joseph two sons: Manasseh and Ephraim.

and played an important role in Joseph fulfilling his own God-ordained purpose. (See Gen. 41:45, 50.)

About Her

Asenath (whose name means "gift of the sun god") was the wife of Joseph, son of Jacob, and the daughter of Potiphera, Egyptian priest of On. She was the mother of Manasseh and Ephraim, each of whom was a father of one of the tribes of Israel.

Apply Her

Be ready for God to use you to help those you love realize their destinies. And in the process, He will lead you to apprehend your own.

Find Her

Genesis 41:45–52
Genesis 46:20

I AM
Shiphrah

And he said, When ye do the office of a midwife to the Hebrew women, and see them upon the stools; if it be a son, then ye shall kill him: but if it be a daughter, then she shall live.

Exodus 1:16

*M*y name is Shiphrah and I am a Hebrew midwife. My job is to deliver healthy lives into this world. Pharaoh, who long oppressed my people and kept them enslaved, demanded that all male, Hebrew newborns be put to death. Pharaoh had observed how quickly the Hebrew people were multiplying and he feared what these baby boys would do when they became men. (Pharaoh spared the baby girls. I guess he didn't fear what infant girls would do when they grew into Hebrew women. He seemed to think they could do him no harm.)

I may not have the strength of a man, but I chose to honor God. Puah, a fellow midwife, and I secretly refused to aid Pharaoh in his sinful decree. We were more afraid of sinning against God than we were of Pharaoh.

When Pharaoh discovered that many Hebrew boys survived, he summoned Puah and I and demanded we tell him why. We told him the Hebrew women gave birth so quickly that midwives could not arrive before the birth. I guess Pharaoh never considered we would dare go against him, so he believed what we told him. Because of our refusal to enter in to Pharaoh's evil scheme, the nation of Israel multiplied.

I would have gladly served God without reward; but Puah and I found favor with Him and He protected us. Pharaoh underestimated the power of God-fearing women who were brave enough to stand on the side of God.

Why Her?

Joseph was a Jewish man who became a ruler in Egypt—second only to Pharaoh. Because of Joseph's wisdom during days of famine, the Jews were welcome in Egypt. But a new Pharaoh arose in Egypt who did not know Joseph. He was fearful of the Jews because they outnumbered the Egyptians. Prompted by his fear, he enslaved all the Jews within his kingdom. But even when they were enslaved, they multiplied. So, Pharaoh decided to kill their first-born males so the Jews would not have the male strength to rise up against him.

> Shiphrah and Puah were midwives who oversaw the delivery of babies to Hebrew women.

Shiphrah and Puah were midwives who oversaw the delivery of babies to Hebrew women. (In those days, there were no hospitals; so midwives went to women's homes to deliver their babies.) Scripture does not make it completely clear whether Shiphrah and Puah were Hebrews or just took care of Hebrew women. However, for whatever reason, the Pharaoh believed they would be capable of killing all the male, Hebrew children and charged them to do so.

These women would not follow Pharaoh's decree; they let all the newborn boys live. But it was not their incapacity for harming these infants that was the motivation for their refusal; it was their fear of God. The Bible says, "the fear of the Lord is the beginning of wisdom" (Ps. 111:10). Shiphrah made her wise decision based on her belief that whatever she might suffer at the hands of Pharaoh for not carrying out his orders would not be as bad as displeasing God.

As it turns out, when these two midwives were questioned by Pharaoh, they were able to give him a story he believed as to why the Jews were still multiplying. And because they chose to please God, He rewarded them.

About Her

It is unclear whether Shiphrah was Egyptian or Hebrew. Nothing is known of her genealogy. We know only that God rewarded her because she feared Him; so He gave her descendants.

The Bible says, "the fear of the Lord is the beginning of wisdom." (Psalm 111:10)

Apply Her

There is nothing on this earth that man can do to us that is worth disobeying or displeasing God. Although God is slow to anger (Ps. 103:8), our relationship to Him should not be based upon punishment or reward but on our love for Him that makes us want to please Him.

Find Her

Exodus 1:15–21

I AM
Miriam

*For I brought thee up out of the
land of Egypt, and redeemed
thee out of the house of servants;
and I sent before thee Moses,
Aaron, and Miriam.*

Micah 6:4

I am Miriam, and I messed up big time. In my time, women rarely had a place of honor and authority; but I did, along with my little brother, Moses, and my other brother, Aaron. People listened to what we said.

It was undeniable that Moses was a prophet of God; but I questioned whether he was the only one who heard from God. I felt I had something to say, too. I certainly didn't think it was right that he married that Ethiopian woman; she was a foreigner to us. So both Aaron and I questioned Moses and his authority.

God didn't like it when Aaron and I questioned the authority of the one He anointed. He told us in no uncertain terms that He alone ordains authority, and Moses was His choice. As a result of my rebellious attitude, God afflicted me with leprosy. But I thank Moses that he cried unto the Lord for my healing, and God heard his prayers.

Seven days later, I was returned to my people healed and whole. God remembered me! To this day, He lists me as one that He sent. I have been forgiven and cleansed, and God remembers my sin of rebellion no more.

Why Her?

When Pharaoh decreed the death of all Hebrew babies, Moses' mother put the infant Moses in a basket and sent him down the Nile River, hoping to save his life. Pharaoh's daughter found Moses floating on the Nile and took him as her own child. God used Miriam, Moses older sister, to suggest he be cared for by a Hebrew—his own mother. As a result, Moses received the loving care of his mother; yet, he was protected from Pharoah's evil scheme to kill all the Jewish sons. By looking out for her brother, Miriam unknowingly played a part in God's plan to use Moses to break the yoke of slavery on Israel and fulfill the prophecy that Israel would be free.

Miriam herself was a leader and called a prophetess. She was highlighted as singing and praising God after He delivered the Israelites by parting the Red Sea. But Miriam was representative of Israel—sometimes she was faithful; other times, she made mistakes and even offended God. Yet, Miriam persevered and learned her lessons well.

Miriam herself was a leader and called a prophetess. She was highlighted as singing and praising God beside the Red Sea.

As a result, God granted her respect and acclaim that has endured throughout the centuries.

About Her

As the daughter of Levites, Jochebed and Amram, Miriam began life as a Hebrew slave in Egypt. She had never known the joy or responsibility of leading her own life through her own choices and decisions. But God called her brother, Moses, to lead Israel out of bondage to Egypt. She lived the rest of her life as a free woman—set free by the power of God.

Apply Her

Like Miriam, we have been set free from slavery—the slavery to sin. God has set us on a new course, and we must learn a new way of life and follow Him faithfully as He leads us. As God brought respect and acclaim to Miriam, He will use us to bring honor and glory to Him.

Find Her

Exodus 2:1–9

Exodus 15:19–21

Numbers 12:1–11

Numbers 20:1

I AM
Pharaoh's Daughter

*And the child grew, and she brought
him unto Pharaoh's daughter, and
he became her son. And she called
his name Moses: and she said,
because I drew him out of the water.*

Exodus 2:10

53

A king in Egypt is called a Pharaoh. I am the daughter of the Pharaoh of my time. I had all access to my father's palace; but I had no husband and no children. One day, I heard a baby crying from a basket floating in the water and caught in the reeds. When I picked him up, I knew I wanted to keep him as my own. But I knew he was a Hebrew boy and my father had ordered all newborn, Hebrew males to be killed. So I got a Hebrew woman, named Jochebed, to wet nurse him until he was weaned. Then I raised him as my own, naming him Moses.

I knew how my father felt about the Hebrews; but Moses was just an innocent child. I saw no reason for him to suffer the consequences of my father's prejudice. I gave Moses all the benefits of being raised as royalty: the best education, the best care, the best training. I did not know at the time that, although I was a pagan, the God of Abraham used me to assist in freeing the Jews from the bondage they lived under during my father's rule in Egypt. The baby I drew from the water became their liberator.

Why Her?

Pharaoh's daughter plays a very important role in the Bible. She was used by God to save the life of Moses.

In her day, Pharaoh had issued a decree that all Hebrew infants were to be killed. To save his life, Moses' family set him adrift in a basket on the Nile River. One day while Pharaoh's daughter was bathing in the Nile, she found the basket containing the tiny, Hebrew, baby boy floating in the water. Pharaoh's daughter had compassion for the baby and decided to raise him as her own. She paid a Hebrew woman (his birth mother) to nurse him and care for him until he was weaned. When the child was older, he was returned to her. She named him Moses, saying, "Because I drew him out of the water" (Ex. 2:10).

In a time of racial prejudice and injustice, Pharaoh's daughter had great courage; not only did she save Moses' life, she accepted him as her own child. Although she was not a believer in the Hebrew God, she was used mightily by Him (See Ex. 2:5–10).

In a time of racial prejudice and injustice, Pharaoh's daughter had the courage to save and adopt Moses.

About Her

Pharaoh's daughter is unnamed; but many believe that her father, the Pharaoh, was Ramses II, who ruled from 1301 through 1234 B.C.

Apply Her

God can use each of us to carry out His plan whether we belong to Him or not. But, like Pharaoh's daughter, we are all called to have compassion for the smallest and weakest, the poor, the infirm, and the old. This is the calling of every person.

Find Her

Exodus 2:5–10
Acts 7:20–22
Hebrews 11:24–25

I AM
Zipporah

*Then Zipporah took a sharp
stone, and cut off the foreskin
of her son, and cast it at his
feet, and said, Surely a bloody
husband art thou to me.*

Exodus 4:25

I, Zipporah, am a Cushite, a descendant of Ham and a Black woman living in Ethiopia.

Moses, who was Hebrew, fled from Egypt after Pharaoh discovered he had killed an Egyptian in defense of a Hebrew slave. My sisters and I were fetching water and Moses rescued us from being hassled and helped us water our flock. When we got home, we told our father, Reuel (called Jethro), what had happened. He asked why we had not brought Moses home.

We went back and got Moses. He and my father really bonded, so much so that I was given to Moses in marriage by my father. After all the people who wanted to kill Moses had died, I travelled back to Egypt with him. It was at that time that God threatened Moses' life, and I had to take matters into my own hands. You see, our son, Gershom, had not been circumcised, as the Hebrew law requires. Moses had failed to obey God. The whole thing created major drama for me. I didn't want God to punish Moses, so I stepped up and circumcised our son myself. Although I was married to one of the greatest men of the Bible, it was, nonetheless, my role to back up my husband and stand in the gap for him. It was abhorrent to me to cut my own son; but I did what needed to be done to save my husband and get things right with God.

Why Her?

The name Zipporah means "a small bird." Zipporah was one of the seven daughters of Reuel (also called Jethro), a Midianite priest. We know little about Zipporah, but the Bible depicts her favorably.

Moses fled Egypt after killing an Egyptian for harming a Hebrew. He traveled to a land just east of Egypt where the people were descendants of Abraham. There, he met and married Zipporah. They had two sons, Gershom and Eliezer.

Moses took some flack from his family for marrying Zipporah. In particular, his sister Miriam and his brother Aaron were jealous of the position that God had given to Moses and spoke against the ethnicity of Zipporah in their jealousy. God heard their pettiness and called them out on it.

As it turns out, Zipporah was the perfect mate for Moses. She was a true helpmate to him when the Lord almost killed him for disobediently failing to circumcise his son. It was Zipporah who stepped up and did

Zipporah was the perfect mate for Moses and was a true help-mate to him when Moses had failed to circumcise their son.

it. Her quick thinking, determination, and obedience to do what God required opened the way for Moses to become the deliverer of the Hebrew people.

About Her

Zipporah was married to Moses and was one of seven daughters born to Reuel (called Jethro), the Midianite. She was the mother of Gershom and Eliezer.

Apply Her

No matter how big and strong and powerful and seemingly invincible the men in our lives might to be, they need our prayers and our actions to support them. They may be our husbands, our brothers, or our friends; they may even be in the military. No matter who they are, they are human. Occasionally, they will slip and fall, and it is up to those of us who love them to pick them up and stand in the gap for them.

Find Her

Exodus 2:15–22

Exodus 4:18–26

Exodus 18:1–6

Numbers 12:1–2

I AM
Elisheba

And Aaron took him Elisheba,
daughter of Amminadab, sister
of Naashon, to wife; and she
bare him Nadab, and Abihu,
Eleazar, and Ithamar.

Exodus 6:23

I am Elisheba, wife of Aaron and sister-in-law of Moses and Miriam. There is not much written about me in the Scriptures, but I am a woman who was highly favored and blessed of the Lord. My name means "God is my Oath."

I considered it an honor to be Aaron's wife. He was such a great man of God. I was also blessed to be the mother of his four sons, Nadab, Abihu, Eleazar, and Ithamar. Each of our sons became a leader of the Levites. Our daughters were trained to serve the Lord.

The Levites were set apart from the other tribes of Israel to be a royal priesthood; they were called to serve God in the tabernacle. As priests of God, the Levites didn't possess land or other material riches. The Levitical inheritance was the priesthood. Yet God provided for us abundantly through the tithes of the other tribes of Israel. The Levites also had the privilege of partaking of the holy offerings—the sacrifices made to God. Not just the men, but also my daughters and I were allowed this holy honor.

Being a good wife and mother was my calling and I helped prepare my daughters and sons to step into the very important roles to which God had called them. Sometimes greatness is found in our service to and discipleship of others. 🖋

Why Her?

Elisheba is mentioned in Scripture to tell of the marriage union of the Levites with the tribe of Judah. Her husband, Aaron, was a Levitical priest. The priests could not inherit nor leave an inheritance. However, Levites could intermarry with women from other tribes because there would be no confusion regarding inheritances, particularly the allocation of land that God had made to each tribe.

Elisheba was from the tribe of Judah—the lineage of Jesus Christ. The union of Elisheba and Aaron created a lineage of kings and priests—a foreshadowing of Jesus who is both King and High Priest.

About Her

Elisheba was the wife of Aaron, the daughter of Amminadab, and the sister of Naashon, all of whom were from the tribe of Judah. Her sons were Nadab, Abihu, Eleazar, and Ithamar.

Elisheba was from the tribe of Judah—the lineage of Jesus Christ.

Apply Her

There are times when we will be remembered only because of the accomplishments of our husbands or our children. We should not take this as a slight, but has a badge of honor! It speaks of our legacy when the family we have loved and nurtured and supported and prayed for has found success! We take a strong hand in that success by being all God called us to be as godly wives and/or mothers.

Find Her

Exodus 6:23

I AM
Tirzah

*And Zelophehad the son of Hepher
had no sons, but daughters: and
the names of the daughters of
Zelophehad were Mahlah, and
Noah, Hoglah, Milcah, and Tirzah.*

Numbers 26:33

*M*y father, Zelophehad had five daughters and no sons. This was a sad thing for a man because, in those days, daughters could not inherit or carry on the family name; daughters would eventually marry and become part of their husband's family.

My sisters and I were bold in our faith and bold in demanding what we wanted. I guess you could say we were among the first to demand equal rights for women. We campaigned to Moses that we should be able to inherit our father's property because, otherwise, his family name would die out. Moses was progressive to even take our request to God.

Amazingly, God told Moses to grant our petition. The only catch was that we had to marry men from our own tribe, so the land we inherited would remain tribal property. That was fair enough. Each of my sisters and I found men from our tribe to marry and inherited the property of our father.

Once again, God showed up and changed the minds of men, proving women truly hold a place in God's kingdom. Through His actions toward us, God reminded us that He loves us all.

Why Her?

Tirzah and her sisters were extraordinarily strong women for their time. They did not accept their place as non-inheritors of their father. They realized that, if they had no inheritance, the existence of their father's family would be wiped out of Israel's genealogy forever.

It was unheard of for women to inherit anything. So it was shocking that God Himself ordained that the inheritance of Zelophehad was to be passed to his daughters. Given the marginalization of women in that culture, it was just as shocking that any man would consider allowing a woman to inherit, even when instructed by God. But Moses did. This is really a testament to how personal God was to people of this generation. God was not an abstract concept to them; He was a real king to them, and they obeyed—even when what He commanded was not what they wanted.

The women of this long-ago day had to marry within their father's family in order to keep their inheritance. This made perfect sense because God

It was unheard of for women to inherit anything. It was shocking that God Himself ordained the inheritance of Zelophehad's daughters.

had already determined and distributed certain land to certain tribes. If the women had married outside of their father's family, the land would have fallen into the hands of their husband's tribe.

About Her

Tirzah was the youngest of Zelophehad's daughters. Zelophehad came from the people of Gilead, was the son of Machir, son of Manasseh, from the clans of the people of Joseph.

Apply Her

Man's rules don't mean anything to God. He will turn the entire world to fit the design of our lives that He ordains. All we have to be is obedient. That is not always easy when God asks us to do or be what we don't want to do or be. But God is trustworthy and worthy to be praised. Nothing He asks us to do will return void.

Find Her

Numbers 26:33
Numbers 27:1–12

Numbers 36
Joshua 17:1–3

I AM

Rahab

By faith the harlot Rahab
perished not with them that
believed not, when she had
received the spies with peace.

Hebrews 11:31

*I*t is true that I am a woman with a bad reputation—a harlot. As low as I was in society, God had a great plan for my place in His kingdom.

My whole life changed when two Hebrew spies came to stay at my house. They had come to spy out the land of Jericho where I lived. Someone told the King of Jericho where they were, and he commanded me to send them out. But I had heard all the God of Israel had done, like parting the Red Sea when the Jews left Egypt. I believed in their God and that He had given them this land. So, I hid the spies under the stalks of flax on my roof and told the king's men that they had left.

I asked the two spies to remember the kindness I showed them and to save me and my family when they conquered Jericho. They agreed to save everyone in my home if I would keep their business to myself and if I would hang a red rope from my window when they invaded the city.

When the Israelites took control of Jericho, they kept their promise to me—they took everyone from my house to safety before they burned down the city. We would have perished with the rest of Jericho if I hadn't believed on the God of Israel and also turned that belief into action.

But my story doesn't end there. I, a harlot on whom God had mercy, am a direct, earthly ancestor of our Lord and Savior, Jesus Christ!

Why Her?

The nation of Israel doubted many times what God had promised. They had been promised Jericho, but doubted that it would ever be theirs. Joshua sent spies into the big city because he was certain God would give them victory over the inhabitants and possession of the "land flowing with milk and honey"—the Promised Land. But, it took Rahab, a Canaanite and a prostitute, to demonstrate to God's people that His promises are real.

Rahab believed God's people would prevail. When she hid the spies, she witnessed to them that she "knew" God had given them the land. At that moment, she became a woman of faith; even as God's people had become faithless. Rahab lived an obviously sinful life, but when she acknowledged Him as her God, He protected her, accepted her as His daughter, and made her life a channel of blessing through the ages. But when she acknowledged Him as her God, He protected her, accepted her as His daughter, and made her life a channel of blessing through the ages. God

Rahab lived an obviously sinful life, but when she acknowledged Him as her God, He protected her, accepted her as His daughter, and he made her life a channel of blessing through the ages.

rewarded her lineage and blessed it as Jesus Christ Himself is one of her descendants.

About Her

Rahab was a Canaanite and a prostitute whose people were at war with Israel. The Canaanites were pagans; yet Rahab acknowledged the one true God. She asked for and received Israel's protection over herself and her family when Israel came into the land that God promised them.

Apply Her

It doesn't matter who we are, where we are, or what we've done; God has a plan for our lives that transcends it all. Like Rahab, sometimes we have to go God's way even when no one around us follows Him. We have to rely on our knowledge of Him and not on what others say or do. God will work first in our lives so we can help lead others to Him.

Find Her

Joshua 2

Joshua 6:16–25

Matthew 1:1–5

Hebrews 11:31

James 2:24–26

I AM

Achsah

And Caleb said, He that smiteth Kirjathsepher, and taketh it, to him will I give Achsah my daughter to wife.

Judges 1:12

*M*y name is Achsah (it means "ankle brace-let"). These days, you might call me a trophy wife. But in my day, that didn't mean you were the most beautiful (although my father gave me my name because he thought I was beautiful); it meant that your father was wealthy and would provide your husband with many of his resources. Well, my father, Caleb, was very wealthy and men wanted to marry me. My father promised the man who was able to take down the city of Debir (once called Kirjathsepher) would win my hand in marriage. He also promised to shower that man with many gifts.

My father's nephew, Othniel, won my hand. But Othniel didn't take the initiative; so I went to my father and negoti-ated my own dowry. Obviously, I knew my father's riches, so I knew what to ask for that would have the most value. In the end, my father gave my betrothed the upper and lower springs. The dowry might not sound like much, but it was water in the desert.

Don't ever under-estimate the power of a woman. I understood the riches that my father held for me, and I used that understanding to get my father to bless my family. Behind many successful men stand women like me—women who are wise and resourceful teammates, helping their men to succeed.

Why Her?

Achsah had been raised with faith and privilege and was used to living well. Her father, Caleb, needed to find a man who could defeat the last of his enemies; and, at the same time, he wanted to find a man who was spiritually and physically strong enough to carry the great weight and wealth of his family into future generations. Othniel was the man and his daughter, Achsah, was the prize.

Othniel was not a weak man. So that is not why his wife went to Caleb instead of him. Caleb had already given the couple a great deal of land, even though it was dry. Achsah was close to her father and knew the best way to approach him to get more. (Achsah appeared to have been Caleb's only daughter and the apple of his eye.) So Achsah did not shy away or take a weak step when it was time to do her part for her family and future generations. She boldly approached her father.

Achsah did not shy away or take a weak step when it was time to do her part for her family and future generations.

About Her

Achsah was the daughter of Caleb and the wife of Othniel, Caleb's brother. Caleb and Joshua were the only two spies who went over to check out the Promised Land and came back with good reports. Because he was a great man of faith, when he went to Joshua to get his portion, he was well rewarded with Hebron, a mountainous land. Achsah's siblings were Iru, Elah, and Naam.

Apply Her

We must approach our heavenly Father as boldly as Achsah approached Caleb. Like Achsah, sometimes we will be called to be our husbands' helpmate (Gen. 2:18). But that doesn't always mean we will take a back seat. Helping sometimes means that we have to step up and act in our areas of strength to support our husbands.

Find Her

Joshua 15:16–19   1 Chronicles 2:48–49
Judges 1:12–15

I AM
Deborah

And Deborah, a prophetess,
the wife of Lapidoth, she
judged Israel at that time.

Judges 4:4

I am Deborah, a prophetess and the only woman to hold the position of judge in Old Testament times.

Once again, Israel had become disobedient to God. As a result, they had been severely oppressed by the Canaanites for twenty years.

God told me to deploy our troops against Canaan, and He would give us victory. But their forces were stronger and our general, Barak, was running scared. I reminded him that the Lord had called him to gather up 10,000 men and go to Mount Tabor, into battle. Barak was foolish; he said he wouldn't go unless I went with him. "Fine," I told him; but I also let him know that, because of his weakness, no glory would come to him for the victory.

As a woman, I could not go into battle myself, but I could speak encouraging words over those who were going onto the battlefield; I could also fight powerfully in the spiritual realm. As Barak prepared to enter into battle, I prophetically assured him that the Lord would go before him, and the battle would be His. Sure enough, Barak and his league of 10,000 men defeated the entire, powerful, Canaanite army. Unfortunately, Barak's lack of confidence in God had caused him to need my presence in battle. As a result, God allowed Sisera, the fearsome Canaanite commander, to escape—Barak lost out on the glory of vanquishing the Canaanite leader. But God's justice was soon served when the fleeing Sisera was killed by Jael, another fearless woman of God.

Why Her?

Deborah was a judge and a prophetess in Israel. In her day, judges were singular authorities who were empowered by God to judge His people in worldly matters. Deborah is the only Old Testament woman who was granted such power. By combining her judging responsibilities with her gift of prophecy, Deborah could not only judge any present situation, but she also infused power and authority into the directions, punishments, and rewards she gave.

Deborah's strong faith made her a spiritual warrior; but God sent her into human battle when He told her to raise up an army of 10,000 against Sisera, the captain of Jabin's army. She called on Barak to lead the army; but Barak was weak and would not go unless Deborah went with him. What a testimony to the trust he had in her that he needed her in the battlefield to win. Prophetically, she knew Barak was weak and that his weakness would cause the honor for the victory to go to Jael, the woman who killed Sisera.

Deborah's strong faith made her a spiritual warrior.

About Her

Deborah was the wife of Lapidoth. (Some interpret that she was from Lippidoth.)

Apply Her

Our jobs and our giftings may not be the same; but like Deborah, when we use our giftings in our everyday responsibilities, we will begin to walk in God's purposes. When we do, the outcome will always have power, and we will be victorious in the kingdom of God.

Find Her

Judges 4:4–14
Judges 5:1–31

I AM

Jael

Blessed above women shall Jael the wife of Heber the Kenite be, blessed shall she be above women in the tent.

Judges 5:24

I am a woman of honor; but make no mistake about it, I am not one to be messed with. I have a gentle, giving, feminine spirit and have been called most blessed of women; but I have a mind of my own.

When Sisera, captain of Jabin's army, came to our tent looking for refuge, I let him in because my husband, Heber, the Kenite, got along with him. Sisera was thirsty and asked me for water, but I went above and beyond and gave him precious milk, instead. I could also see he needed rest, so I gave him a blanket to cover himself.

Although Sisera thought he was safe in the tent of a harmless woman, I knew who he was. I was more than aware of his reputation as a zealous oppressor of the Israelites. He was an enemy, not my friend.

So, while he rested, I picked up a nail and a hammer; I hammered the nail into his head and killed him. Little did I know that it had been prophesied that he would die that very day by the hand of a woman. I was used to defeat an enemy of Israel.

Just because I am a woman of honor and a servant, don't think I am powerless. To the contrary, I am my own woman, empowered by God.

Why Her?

Jael quietly and without boasting or fanfare took out a very powerful man. The man was an enemy of Israel named Sisera, a general over the Canaanite army, second only to the king. Jael did what Israel's army could not do—kill Sisera. We do not know exactly why she killed Sisera, since her husband did work for King Jabin. But we do know Jael descended from priests. Sisera had no business in the tent of a married woman, and Jael was quick to turn his body over to Barak, who led Israel's army. Most importantly, we know God's will was done that day as Deborah had prophesied, "for the Lord shall sell Sisera into the hand of a woman" (Judg. 4:9).

Deborah called Jael "blessed above women." The only other woman in the Bible who is called this special name is Jesus' mother, Mary.[1] So, what does Jael have in common with Mary that she would be called "blessed above women?" Whether conscious of it or not, Jael was a willing

---

1 Judith is called blessed in the Catholic book of Judith. Also, Mary's blessing is a divine blessing, and Jael's is meant to be a heroic title.

God's will was done that day as Deborah had prophesied, "for the Lord shall sell Sisera into the hand of a woman." (Judges 4:9)

vessel whom God used to accomplish His purpose. In Judges 4:23 it is clear that it was God who "subdued on that day Jabin the king of Canaan before the children of Israel."

About Her

Jael was not an Israelite; she was a Kenite, married to Heber. She was a descendant of Moses' father-in-law, who was a priest.

Apply Her

If God wants to use us, we must let Him. Any of us may find that we will be called "blessed among women."

Find Her

Judges 4:9–22
Judges 5:6, 23–27

I AM
Delilah

And when Delilah saw that he had told her all his heart, she sent and called for the lords of the Philistines, saying, Come up this once, for he hath shewed me all his heart. Then the lords of the Philistines came up unto her, and brought money in their hand.

Judges 16:18

*S*amson thought he was a player, but I had a surprise for him! He had a reputation as a big strong man—he even tore a lion apart with his bare hands. But I'd also heard all about him lying with prostitutes and the like. Then he started trying to talk to me! Actually, he fell in love with me, but I felt nothing for him. He was merely an opportunity for me to make some money.

The rulers of the Philistines told me they would each give me eleven hundred pieces of silver if I could find out the secret of Samson's great strength. I just asked him directly what would make him weak. He kept telling me false answers; and each time I tried to take away his strength, I failed.

Finally, I played the if-you-loved-me-you'd-confide-in-me card, and he spilled the beans. He told me that if his hair was cut he would lose his super strength and become like other men. Fool that he was, he betrayed his special talents and calling. He trusted his fate to someone like me—a woman who believed none of the things he believed. In the end, Samson lost it all.

Why Her?

The story of Samson and Delilah has been portrayed by the world as a great and passionate love story. But there was no love in it—only lust, greed, and the attempt of the devil to keep Israel in bondage to the Philistines.

Samson was set apart by God for greatness; but Samson foolishly gave in to his sinful desires. One of those desires came in the form of Delilah, the cold hearted seductress. Delilah was an opportunist and only out for herself. She didn't consider the consequences her actions would have on anyone else. Her selfish motivation was money. Delilah even had the nerve to get angry when Samson would not cooperate with her deceptions, which interfered with her collection of thousands of silver pieces. One of the saddest parts of this story is that Delilah was so busy living a selfish life she never knew the purposes for which God created her. She exemplifies someone who allowed, and even invited, the enemy to use her for his schemes as she took down the great, strong man, Samson.

It seemed Delilah's scheming had destroyed Samson as he suffered greatly at the hands of Delilah and her co-conspirators. But the story does not end there. Samson was blinded and his strength taken; but it was only when these trappings of apparent piety were taken away that he became a great man of faith. In the end, he fulfilled the purposes for which God had ordained him, and in an act of martyrdom, took down thousands of Philistines.

About Her

It is no coincidence that the Bible tells us nothing of Delilah's lineage—we are told nothing of a husband or descendants. We don't even know about her death. She lived life on her own terms and not God's way; so her life was wasted and her legacy cut off.

Apply Her

We must not be used by the devil. We cannot become part of his scheme. If we are not living our lives for Christ and serving others, then we are assisting the enemy. We must not be on the wrong side of eternity. When God has set His own plan in motion, we will be helpless to defeat it anyway. And if we are unrepentant in our actions against God's plan, we will have sealed our own fates.

Find Her

Judges 16:4–21

I AM

Ruth

*And Ruth said, Intreat me not to
leave thee, or to return from following
after thee: for whither thou goest, I
will go; and where thou lodgest, I
will lodge: thy people shall be my
people, and thy God my God.*

Ruth 1:16

I am the great-grandmother of David, the mighty king of Israel. Of course, I couldn't know that when I was living; but now I know that I am part of his spiritual heritage.

It was in my grief over losing my husband and watching my mother-in-law lose her sons that I, a Moabite woman, came to know Jehovah God. My mother-in—law, Naomi, had qualities of love and strength that made me know her God was real. So after my husband died and Naomi decided to leave Moab and return to her homeland, I had to go with her. I knew that I had to stay with this godly woman.

I worked out my grief with hard toil in the fields of Judah. I was a poor widow with no one to provide for me or pro-tect me. But Naomi and I looked out for each other. It was a difficult time, but my dedication to my mother-in-law demanded I stay and hope for a better future. I never gave a thought to marrying again, particularly in a land where I was a foreigner. So I just continued to work hard and be a support to Naomi. But when the time was right, Boaz came into my life. God had plans for me that prospered me and gave me hope and a future.

Why Her?

Ruth is the picture of loyalty and love. She honored her mother-in-law, Naomi; so much that, in the grief of mourning her husband's death, she moved with Naomi to Israel. Moabites were hated in Israel. Yet, Ruth pledged her life to Naomi, even though it was unlikely that she would find happiness in Israel. For what Jewish man would marry a Moabitess in his own land? But Ruth was not just following after Naomi, she was also following after Naomi's God; for she said, "and your god, my god" (Ruth 1:16).

God blessed Ruth for her selfless acts and her new found faith, which grew to great faith. But Ruth was humble. She did nothing but serve Naomi and work hard in the fields; and she was thankful when Boaz showed kindness to her. This Moabitess did marry Boaz, an Israelite man of her husband's lineage; and she became the great-grandmother of David.

God blessed Ruth for her selfless acts and her new found faith, which grew to great faith.

About Her

Ruth was born a Moabite and was the widow of Naomi's son. She married Boaz, Naomi's kinsman and Rahab's son. She is one of only two women who have books of the Bible about them. The other book is Esther.

Apply Her

God rewards the steadfast, hard-working, and faithful women of faith who serve Him and those around them. If we want the best of God's blessings, we have to take our focus off of ourselves and put it onto someone else.

Find Her

Ruth 1:2–22

Ruth 2

Ruth 3

Ruth 4

I AM
Naomi

And Naomi said unto her two daughters in law, Go, return each to her mother's house: the Lord deal kindly with you, as ye have dealt with the dead, and with me.

Ruth 1:8

*M*y husband, my two sons, and I moved to Moab after a famine hit our land of Judah. After my husband died, my sons both married Moabite women. They did not believe as we believed, but I loved them both dearly. About ten years later, both my sons also died. I was grief stricken. So I took my two daughters-in-law and headed back to Israel.

But I became concerned for those two young women. I told them to go back to Moab and find new husbands because I had nothing to offer them. I was just a bitter old woman; I was so bitter that I changed my name from Naomi, meaning pleasant and agreeable, to Mara, meaning bitter. Neither of them wanted to leave me, but I insisted. One went back, but Ruth refused and decided to stay with me and adopt my God. What a loyal woman!

It was in my homeland of Judah that she met and married (with a little matchmaking from me) Boaz, my kinsman. They had a son, who was my own blood, continuing my family line.

Ruth could have abandoned me and let me wallow in my bitterness, but she would not. It was through Ruth's loyalty and the birth of my grandson, Obed, that I was healed from my grief and my bitterness returned to sweetness.

Why Her?

Naomi is Hebrew for "pleasant." But after moving from her homeland of Israel to Moab, Naomi's husband and both of her sons died within only ten years; and she had no grandchildren. Naomi was grief stricken. She decided to return to Israel. Naomi's Moabite daughters-in-law followed behind because of her great faith, but Naomi had become hopeless. She told people not to call her Naomi anymore, but to call her Mara, instead. Mara is Hebrew for "bitter."

At the root of Naomi's bitterness was sadness because she perceived that God had brought all the devastation to her life. She believed her life was over, with no more meaning or purpose. All she knew to do was to pack up and go back to Israel.

Because Naomi had ministered and shown herself to be a true worshipper of God, her daughter-in-law, Ruth, refused to let her give up on herself or God. Ruth clung to Naomi and dedicated herself to serving her.

This is a wonderful reminder that, even when we are faithless, God continues to be faithful. When all seemed lost for establishment of Naomi's family, Ruth and Boaz, a kinsman from Naomi's own bloodline, married and had a child; a child who is counted as Naomi's own lineage. Joy was restored to Naomi's life.

About Her

Naomi is the widow of Elimelech, and mother of Chilion (married to Orpah) and Mahlon (married to Ruth).

Apply Her

Historically, African American women are well acquainted with how close an extended family, and even non-blood kinship, can be. During the time of slavery, when a child was sold off to another plantation, a woman at that plantation would suckle the child, love her, raise her, and call her family.

That concept should not be lost on the current generations. It is the blood of Jesus that binds us all as family. As we are filled with the Holy Spirit, we must not hold back from pouring all we have out on others. If we hold nothing back, we will surely be refilled to overflowing.

Find Her

Ruth 1:2–22   Ruth 3

Ruth 2   Ruth 4

I AM
Hannah

But unto Hannah he gave a worthy
portion; for he loved Hannah: but
the Lord had shut up her womb.
And her adversary also provoked her
sore, for to make her fret, because
the Lord had shut up her womb.

1 Samuel 1:5–6

I wanted nothing more than to have children; but I never conceived. I was barren. I can't tell you how much pain I felt in my childlessness. To make matters worse, my husband's other wife, Penninah, had borne him children. And boy, did she rub it in every chance she got.

I often asked myself what I had done wrong. Why had I been burdened with being barren? People looked at me with such judgment. They obviously thought me sinful for God to have brought such a curse upon me. My husband often told me how much he loved me whether or not I could have children; but I couldn't receive what he said.

Finally, when I could stand the pain no more, I prayed to the Lord and wept bitterly before Him. I promised if God would grant me a son, I would give him back for service to Him. Something happened when I took my cares directly to God. And after that, I was a new, bolder Hannah.

The Lord blessed me with Samuel. I did as I promised and gave him into the Lord's service. Although it broke my mother's heart to let go of my son, the Lord blessed me with three more children. If I learned nothing else, I learned to not brood over my life but to take my cares to the Lord in prayer.

Why Her?

Elkanah really loved Hannah; but God had shut up her womb (which means it was God's will, at the time, for her to not have children). Having children in those days was an indication of status, stature, and blessing; so, although it was not the plan of God, Elkanah took another wife, Peninnah, to bear his children. This caused Elkanah to have a divided house, one with strife and high drama. Hannah couldn't have children so she was miserable and Penninah rubbed Hannah's barrenness in her face.

Finally, out of her misery, Hannah prayed and prayed, and never gave up praying or believing that God would one day give her a child. God did answer her prayers and Hannah kept her promise: she gave her son, Samuel, over to the service of God. To honor her for keeping her promises, God blessed her with five more children.

About Her

Hannah was from Ramah and was married to Elkanah, the son of Jehoram. She was the mother of Samuel, three other sons, and two daughters.

Apply Her

Everybody has a Peninnah—the person in each of our lives with whom we feel we must compete. A Peninnah is a person who rubs our noses in the fact that she seems to have everything we don't have, and she seems to be everything we aren't. We have to learn not to resent people like this, but to bless them; and then we must press harder to be everything God has called each of us to be.

We are commanded to pray without ceasing. When we keep this command, God will not fail to honor our prayers and to answer them in His time, according to His will. As it was with Hannah, God's outcome is always worth the wait.

Find Her

1 Samuel 1
1 Samuel 2

I AM
Peninnah

Now there was a certain man of
Ramathaimzophim, of mount
Ephraim, and his name was
Elkanah, the son of Jeroham, the
son of Elihu, the son of Tohu,
the son of Zuph, an Ephrathite:
And he had two wives; the name
of the one was Hannah, and
the name of the other Peninnah:
and Peninnah had children, but
Hannah had no children.

1 Samuel 1:1–2

*Y*ou've heard stories like this before: two women fighting over one man. The one who has the baby by him wins, right? Wrong.

I was Elkanah's second wife. I knew he loved his first wife, Hannah, but she couldn't give him babies. I could, and I did. Still, he longed for her.

I did everything I could to put Hannah down. I even taunted her, telling her that God Himself had shut up her womb. I tried everything, but my bitterness just increased; my envy made me more envious; and my jealousy made me more jealous. Nothing worked to change the mess I was in, and I was consumed by the evil I wished on others.

Finally, God opened Hannah's womb, and she started to have babies. At the same time, because of my evil, my children began to die. Before they all died, I begged Hannah to ask God not to take any more of my children. When I finally trusted God to fix my mess, He answered Hannah's prayers on my behalf. But look at all I could have avoided if I had gone to Him first.[1]

---

1 In addition to the Old Testament account, this story is embellished from the Midrash which is a type of non-halakhic literary activity of the Rabbis for interpreting non-legal material according to special principles of interpretation (hermeneutical rules) and was taken from Kadari, Tamar. "Peninnah: Midrash and Aggadah." Jewish Women: A Comprehensive Historical Encyclopedia. 20 March 2009. Jewish Women's Archive. January 13, 2012

Why Her?

Although Peninnah was Elkanah's second wife, she was more like the "other woman." Elkanah adored Hannah; but she was barren. So Elkanah had his children with Peninnah. Peninnah knew she was less favored; so she was purposefully mean to Hannah. Peninnah teased Hannah about the fact that she had children with Elkanah and Hannah didn't. Peninnah acted out of jealousy, but even more so, out of disappointment that God seemed to have carved out a pitiful life for her. She wondered why Hannah got all of the love and adoration, and she wondered why she wasn't good enough even when she was the one who produced children for her husband.

About Her

Peninnah was a Zuphite who was one of Elkanah's two wives.

Peninnah knew she was less favored; so she was purposefully mean to Hannah.

Apply Her

We may look at our lots in life and wonder, as
Peninnah did, "Is this all you have for me, Lord?"
The answer is "No," this is not all God has for
any of us. He has for us His highest and best
according to His riches and glory. But, before
God can move any of us forward to "more,"
we have to be good stewards of the situations
God has us living in now. Just as we must be
a good steward with our money, we have to be
able to manage a little before we can manage
a lot. Wherever we now find ourselves, God, in
His ultimate wisdom, knows our situations are
for our good. We must learn to thank Him for
arranging our lives with loving hands and praise
Him for what tomorrow will bring.

Find Her

1 Samuel 1:1–6

I AM
Michal

*And Saul saw and knew that
the Lord was with David, and
that Michal Saul's daughter loved
him. And Saul was yet the more
afraid of David; and Saul became
David's enemy continually.*

1 Samuel 18:28–29

I am Michal, daughter of King Saul. David was a poor man, but I surely did love him. I knew he was originally supposed to marry my sister, Merab, but I felt certain he would come to love me. Marriage to either one of us would bring him power, and my father would bless the marriage because he wanted an alliance with David whom everyone adored. So it would be a win-win for everyone. Or so I thought.

As it turned out, my father used me as bait to try to set David up. In order to win my hand, my father told David he had to do the seemingly impossible: deliver to him one hundred Philistine foreskins. But David succeeded. When David delivered the foreskins, my father felt even more threatened by him and his power than he had before. I think my father was also jealous because he knew how much everyone, including me, loved David.

I knew what my father was capable of, so I warned David that my father intended to kill him; then I helped him escape. My love for David was true; I was willing to do what was best for him and let him go rather than have my father bring him harm. It was my place to support my husband in all things.

Why Her?

Michal was a woman in love with her husband, David. She also loved her father, King Saul. But her husband and father were in conflict with one another. King Saul saw David as a threat to his throne. The truth is that God had already ordained that David would sit on the throne.

David, who once looked up to Saul, realized that Saul had come against him. And there was Michal, right in the middle. As her faith required, Michal supported her husband and helped him escape from her father. And when Saul saw his daughter's love for David, he stopped pursuing her husband.

Unfortunately, there was no happy ending for Michal. David took another wife; so Michal found another husband and lived happily until David, who ascended to the throne, demanded to have Michal back in return for peace with her last remaining brother, Ishbaal. Ishbaal delivered Michal to King David; but Michal despised David in her heart, and she never had children with him.

About Her

Michal was one of King David's wives and was the daughter of King Saul and Ahinoam. She had six siblings, including her older sister, Merab.

Apply Her

If Michal had been able to look ahead and see that David would bring her sorrow, maybe she would not have chosen to support him against her father. But we must follow in Michal's footsteps. Regardless of whether we think our marriages will last, or how close we are to our families, our husbands must always come first. We are to be one with our husbands (Eph. 5:31). We should always stand with them and never against them. We must be faithful to our husbands even if we must choose between them and our parents or siblings.

Find Her

I AM

Abigail

Now the name of the man was
Nabal; and the name of his wife
Abigail: and she was a woman
of good understanding, and of a
beautiful countenance: but the man
was churlish and evil in his doings
and he was of the house of Caleb.

1 Samuel 25:3

*N*abal, my husband, was as mean as they come, and his meanness caused him to do some foolish things. But, there was one time when he totally outdid himself.

David, a great man, protected Nabal's men as they herded our sheep near David's land. But when David humbly sent a request to Nabal to treat his men with the same kindness, Nabal refused. How stupid was that? Even I knew such a refusal would bring the power of the House of David against us.

I felt compelled to smooth things over with David. So I gathered up bread, wine, sheep, and grain to offer David and went to him as his servant in order to save us all.

Fortunately, I got there just in time. David and his men were on their way to kill every male in our camp. I thank God that David was gracious enough to accept my offer. I was able to show him that he did not want blood on his own sword if he could avoid it.

About ten days later, Nabal died. David sent for me and made me his wife. I had been in a bad situation with an evil husband, and I thought there was no way out. But God heard my pleas. He both avenged and blessed me without me lifting a finger, other than to honor my husband as God commanded me to do.

Why Her?

On numerous occasions, the description of Abigail in comparison to Nabal demonstrates that they are polar opposites. Abigail is described as intelligent and good looking, and her husband is brutish and mean.

Many times, even today, we find ourselves in a marriage relationship that is not satisfying. Our husband has not been abusive to us or our children or done anything that would require or legitimize us leaving, but we are just not happy with who he is. Like Abigail, we are called to honor our husbands in this situation. She even asked David to blame her and take out his wrath on her for the disrespect that was shown him. She offered herself as a sacrifice for her husband.

Abigail is a role model for the modern woman because she is an example of how God recognizes and rewards intelligent and resourceful women who exercise their independence in favor of their husbands and not against them. Even one of Nabal's men, after hearing the exchange between Nabal and David's men, brought the problem to Abigail, trusting she was capable of protecting her husband's household when her husband was clueless to the peril he had brought upon their heads by insulting David.

Abigail didn't try to control her husband, but left him to God. God dealt with Nabal and gave the widow, Abigail, a new husband who loved God and respected her wisdom.

At the same time, God rewarded David with a compatible mate who was beautiful, intelligent, and prophetic—a true helpmate.

About Her

Abigail was born in Carmel. After becoming the widow of Nabal, she married King David. She was a prophetess (as she spoke prophetic words to David) and was considered both beautiful and intelligent. She had no children with Nabal, but bore a son with David—Kileab, whose name was changed to Daniel. According to tradition, Abigail died in Jerusalem.

Apply Her

It is not our job to fix or judge anyone else, including our husbands. It us up to us to humbly and submissively follow God in all we do and leave others in His capable hands. God will make it all work for our good.

Find Her

1 Samuel 25:3–43	2 Samuel 2:1–3
1 Samuel 27:2–4	2 Samuel 3:2–3
1 Samuel 30:5	1 Chronicles 3:1–3

I AM

Rizpah

> And Rizpah the daughter of
> Aiah took sackcloth, and spread
> it for her upon the rock, from the
> beginning of harvest until water
> dropped upon them out of heaven,
> and suffered neither the birds of
> the air to rest on them by day, nor
> the beasts of the field by night.

2 Samuel 21:10

I am Rizpah, concubine of the late, King Saul, with whom I had two sons. The lives of my sons were sacrificed to end the famine in Israel by getting absolution from the Gibeonites.

You see, while King David was on the throne, there was a famine. David went to the Lord and asked Him why the famine had come upon the people of Israel. God told him it was because Saul had killed a great number of Gibeonites. So David went to the Gibeonites to ask what they wanted to atone for the deaths of their people. They didn't request gold or silver; they wanted the lives of seven of Saul's descendants.

Both my sons were given into the hands of the Gibeonite king. I might have been able to properly grieve for my sons if they had been killed in battle. But they were hanged and their bodies were left for the birds of prey and beasts to eat.

I could not let my sons and their memory be so insulted and defiled. I spread out sack cloth on a rock near where they lay, and it became my bed for weeks. I watched over my boys as I had when they were children to keep their bodies away from harm. Day and night I stood watch until the rains signaled to me that Saul's sin against Gibeon had been atoned.

King David took pity on me and had the bodies of my sons removed and given to me. I could do nothing more for my sons in life, but in death I could pay them honor.

Why Her?

Rizpah was like every mother who seeks to protect their children, even in death. Rizpah had two sons with King Saul; and when Saul died, Abner, the commander of Saul's army, took Rizpah as his own. Saul's only surviving son, Ishbosheth, confronted Abner about taking his father's woman, and the quarrel between the two resulted in Abner leaving his post as commander. This resulted in David's rise to power against Ishbosheth.

It is ironic that, when David sought to make peace with the Gibeonites (with whom Saul had made war) and they asked for the sacrifice of seven of Saul's sons, it was Rizpah's sons whom David sacrificed. They were killed and their bodies left to rot, which should have been an embarrassment, even to David. It was Rizpah's protection of her sons' bodies, night and day, that drew attention to the horrific manner in which these young men had been dishonored in death for the sins of their father.

Rizpah was like every mother who seeks to protect their children, even in death.

About Her

Rizpah was the concubine of King Saul and the daughter of Aiah. Her sons were Armoni and Mephibosheth.

Apply Her

A mother's protection of her children is never completed. We must guard over them even should their deaths precede ours—protecting their reputations and legacies. We must include ourselves in the long list of mothers throughout history who have stood against the injustices done to their children. We must be diligent— whether it is to sit in, stand up, march around, start a blog, write letters, or like Rizpah, stand watch over them. We all stand with you, my sisters, united for our children.

Find Her

2 Samuel 3:7–8
2 Samuel 21:3–14

I AM
Bathsheba

And it came to pass in an evening tide, that David arose from off his bed, and walked upon the roof of the king's house: and from the roof he saw a woman washing herself; and the woman was very beautiful to look upon.

2 Samuel 11:2

I am Bathsheba, the great love of David's life. I am ashamed to say, our relationship started when I committed adultery with David while I was still married to Uriah (Urias), the Hittite. I even became pregnant by David at that time; but my husband never knew because he was killed soon after. I did mourn him.

As soon as the mourning time was over, King David sent for me and made me his wife. But soon tragedy struck us; the son we had sinfully born took sick and died by the Lord's hand. It was our punishment. But God forgave us and allowed me to bear four more sons for David.

When David was old, his eldest son, Adonijah, made it known to everyone that he would be king and even began to assume the role since David was near death. But David had promised me that our son, Solomon, would be King. So I went to David and took the prophet, Nathan, with me to back me up. We got David to bless Solomon as king.

Later I went to Solomon on Adonijah's behalf to ask if Solomon would allow Adonijah to take one of David's concubines as his wife. I was tricked, but Solomon was not. He knew Adonijah was still trying to take power from him and wanted to use this concubine to help him; so Solomon slew his brother, Adonijah.

Why Her?

Bathsheba was the wife of King David and the mother of King Solomon. She is one of only four women mentioned in the lineage of Christ. As the wife of the king, she was a very important political figure; and her actions tell us she was a very resourceful woman. We often hear about how she became David's wife, but we hear little about how she secured David's throne for her son (1 Kings 1:11–31). David and Bathsheba suffered the consequences of their sin; but when they repented, God appointed their son to be king.

Bathsheba and Nathan, a prophet and adviser to King David, appealed to David when his throne was being threatened by his son, Adonijah. They made David aware of his son's disloyalty and the subsequent threat to Solomon's life. Bathsheba also reminded him of his promise to make Solomon king. David declared that Solomon would be the heir to his throne. Bathsheba's actions saved her son's life and assured that Solomon would reign as king.

About Her

Bathsheba was the wife of Uriah the Hittite and the daughter of Ammiel. After Uriah died, she became the wife of King David and bore him five sons. The son born of her adultery with David died and her son Solomon succeeded David as King of Israel.

Apply Her

God has given us all the wisdom and giftings we need to succeed in life. But if we insist on wallowing in sin without repentance, God may judge us harshly for our sins as He did David and Bathsheba. When we repent of our sins and turn back to Him, He will wash away the past and restore the greatness He intended for our lives, even though we may still have to deal with the consequences of our sinful actions. This restoration can even affect generations to come in much the same manner that it affected Solomon, David and Bathsheba's son, whom God placed on the throne of Israel.

Find Her

2 Samuel 11:2–5, 26–27

2 Samuel 12:9–24

1 Kings 1:11–31

1 Kings 2:12–25

1 Chronicles 3:1–5

Matthew 1:6

I AM

Tamar,

DAVID'S DAUGHTER

*And Absalom her brother said
unto her, Hath Amnon thy
brother been with thee? but hold
now thy peace, my sister: he is
thy brother; regard not this thing.
So Tamar remained desolate in
her brother Absalom's house.*

2 Samuel 13:20

I am Tamar, the daughter of King David and a desolate woman. My half-brother, Amnon, was sick, and my father asked me to take him cakes. I did as I was asked. When I delivered the cakes to Amnon, he asked that I feed him from my hand. When I got close, Amnon grabbed me and asked me to have sex with him. I vehemently refused. I told him that if he had asked our father, he would have given me to Amnon in marriage. But Amnon was on fire with lust; he raped me.

Afterward, he loathingly told me to get out. I begged him not to turn his back on me; if he didn't want me, I would be a disgraced woman. But Amnon didn't care. He had his servant throw me out.

My other brother, Absalom, saw me grieving, realized what had happened, and convinced me to stay quiet about Amnon's sinful behavior. When my father found out he was angry but did nothing. It seemed no one would defend me, and I was eaten alive by this dirty, family secret. Eventually, my brother Absalom avenged me and killed Amnon for what he had done.

I plead with every woman who has been a victim of incest or rape to speak up. Don't be like me and hide the sinful truth, allowing it to eat at your heart as it did mine. Instead, give honor to yourself, even when no one else will.

Why Her?

Tamar was raped by Amnon, her brother, and it did her great harm. Her first pain was the way he dishonored her—as much after the act as in perpetrating it. She knew she was ruined for a husband for the rest of her life unless Amnon were to marry her. His rejection meant she would have no chance of marriage in her future. She felt alone. She marked herself and tore the clothes she wore as a sign of her ruined status. She could wear a virgin's attire no more because she was unclean; she wept as she mourned the loss. Finally, she went into a deep depression and hid herself in her brother Absalom's house out of fear and guilt.

About Her

Tamar was the daughter of King David. She had more than twenty siblings, including half-siblings. Among these were Amnon, David's first born, and Absalom. All we know of Tamar's mother is that she was David's concubine.

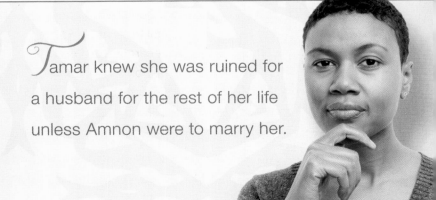

Tamar knew she was ruined for a husband for the rest of her life unless Amnon were to marry her.

Apply Her

Unfortunately, in the days Tamar lived, violent acts against women were a reflection on the woman. Thankfully, today, we call out the crime and blame the criminal.

If you find yourself in Tamar's position, restoration is possible; but it is a process. It may take time, but rest assured, God will heal you and give you hope and peace. Your fate is not sealed because you were a victim; neither is your future defined by it.

Find Her

2 Samuel 13:1–32

1 Chronicles 3:9

I AM

The
Queen of
Sheba

And she came to Jerusalem with a very great train, with camels that bare spices, and very much gold, and precious stones: and when she was come to Solomon, she communed with him of all that was in her heart.

1 Kings 10:2

I was more than curious about this God that the Israelites worship, so I came to meet with Israel's King Solomon. I really wanted to know about his God. To show my sincerity, I came bearing camels, spices, gold, and precious stones to present to him. I put many questions to Solomon and he answered them all. I was stunned by the depth of his wisdom and faith. With all he had and all he was, he still believed in this God who had clearly blessed him richly. On top of that, everyone around him was happy. I would never have believed it except that I saw it with my own eyes.

I blessed this God who put Solomon on the throne of Israel and who blessed that nation with Solomon's leadership and sense of justice. I brought Solomon even more gifts from my country and he gave me an open door to take whatever I wished from his. After I blessed God and Solomon blessed me, I went back to my own country.

Why Her?

The Queen of Sheba, the wealthy and powerful sovereign of a southern nation, heard of King Solomon's wisdom. She traveled to Jerusalem to meet with him and ask him some difficult questions. It was her intention to test him. She was accompanied by a large group of attendants, camels carrying spices and jewels, and a large amount of gold as a gift for the king—her great wealth on display for all to see.

This was the meeting of two heads of state, and it was full of fanfare. The Queen of Sheba came to Jerusalem with something to prove but left with a deep respect for Solomon. This visit also set the stage for trade between the two nations, something that was unusual for this time.

The queen could count this trip a success; not only did she return home with many gifts, but she received the lasting benefit of Solomon's godly wisdom.

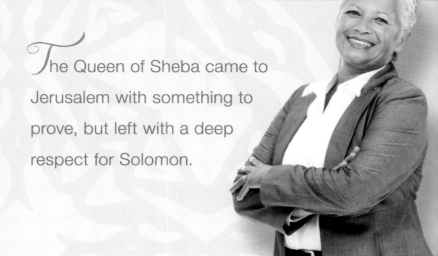

The Queen of Sheba came to Jerusalem with something to prove, but left with a deep respect for Solomon.

About Her

Sheba is the first queen mentioned in the Bible; some say she is from an Ethiopia nation. Others say she was queen of an Arab nation. Jesus mentions her as having gone out of her way to hear Solomon's wisdom.

The wisdom of Christ exceeds all other wisdom, even wisdom like Solomon's. We can seek Christ and His wisdom with open hearts, as the Queen of Sheba sought out Solomon.

Apply Her

No matter whom you are or how much you think you know, humble yourself and seek God's wisdom. The riches gained will be worth far more than the price of your pride.

Find Her

1 Kings 10:1–13
2 Chronicles 9:1–12
Matthew 12:42

I AM

Jezebel

> *And it came to pass that [Ahab] took to wife Jezebel the daughter of Ethbaal king of the Zidonians, and went and served Baal and worshipped him.*

1 Kings 16:31

I am Jezebel, daughter of the King of Zidon and a follower of Baal. I married Ahab, King of Israel, and turned his beliefs to Baal. Some of his people followed suit and worshipped my god, as well. Neither Ahab nor his people were a challenge to my strong will. I got my way with them all.

But one day, Elijah, a prophet of Yahweh, called for a demonstration of power to see whose god was greater. Two bullocks were slaughtered and placed on altars. Baal and the God of Abraham were each called upon to light a fire under the sacrifices. Baal did not answer! Elijah mocked us by pouring water on Yahweh's altar. The fire of his God then fell on the sacrifice, consuming it! Judah's people turned back to their God. And Elijah killed all the prophets of Baal.

I swore revenge on Elijah, but he hid from me. I never got my revenge, but I continued to reign as Queen of Israel, even after Ahab was killed in battle. In the end, Jehu, who sought to take the crown from my son, attacked the palace. I thought I was ready for him, dressed in my most royal attire. But I died in the attack as vainly and defiantly as I lived. 🪶

Why Her?

God's First Commandment says we should have no other gods before Him (Ex. 20:3). And He warns in Deuteronomy 11:6 to "Take heed to yourselves, that your heart be not deceived, and ye turn aside, and serve other gods, and worship them."

Jezebel was the deceiver who enticed Israel to turn from the true God of Abraham toward idol worship of Baal and Astarte. By marrying the King of Israel, Jezebel became an enemy within. Because she had prestige and power, some idly followed her and some were afraid to not follow where she led.

King Ahab himself turned from God to worship Baal. As a result, God made good on His promises and dried up Israel's land. This infuriated Jezebel. So, she persecuted and even killed God's prophets. Big mistake! Ahab died, and Jezebel ascended to the throne of Israel for only a short period. God appointed Jehu, a man after His own heart, to take over leadership of the nation. Jezebel was executed, and her flesh was eaten by dogs.

About Her

Jezebel was married to King Ahab of Israel and was the mother of King Ahaziah, King Jehoram, and a daughter, Athaliah. She was the daughter of the Phoenician king,

Ethbaal I of Tyre and the Sidonians, who was a worshipper of Baal.

Apply Her

Jezebel was born through generations of idol worshippers. Idol worship defined who she was; and she was determined to convert everyone to her way of thinking.

We are accountable to God. We either serve Him or we serve idols such as: money, fame, looks, possessions, or the next, new, popular religion. It is easy to be led astray if we are blindly following someone else or following what the crowd does. We don't want to put our eternity in the hands of mob rule. Follow the One who always does what He says He will do. The One who ultimately died and got back up from the grave! No other idol, god, prophet, or man has ever done that. Only Jesus, by the hand of the true and living God, conquered death.

Find Her

1 Kings 16:30–32
1 Kings 18:4, 13, 19
1 Kings 19: 1–2

1 Kings 21:4–16, 23–25
2 Kings 9:4–10, 22, 30–37
Revelation 2:20–23

I AM
Athaliah

*But when Athaliah the mother
of Ahaziah saw that her son was
dead, she arose and destroyed all the
seed royal of the house of Judah.*

2 Chronicles 22:10

I am the only woman who ever sat on the throne of David; I am Athaliah, daughter of King Ahab and the great Queen Jezebel. I took my strength from my mother, a staunch follower of Baal, and I reigned in Judah for six years.

I married Jehoram, the son of King Jehoshaphat of Judah. My husband reigned over Judah when his father finally died. Though he ruled, Jehoram feared the loss of his throne. To secure his position, he killed all his brothers. In the end, Jehoram died from a terrible disease. My son, Ahaziah, then ascended to the throne; but he was killed in battle a year later.

I grew tired of enduring weak men on the throne. I desired to reign over Judah myself, so I killed all of the royal seed who could take the throne from me. However, I was unaware my husband's daughter had hidden my young grandson, Joash, from me.

One fateful day, I found my daughter had joined forces with a priest and had proclaimed Joash king. What a backstabber! I tried to run in fear of my life, but I was captured and killed. The nation rejoiced at my death and banished Baal worship from Judah.

I abused my power and used it for myself. I was a reflection of the one I worshipped.

Why Her?

What kind of woman would murder her entire family so she could have absolute power? Athaliah was just plain evil. But she wasn't just evil by herself; she led others away from God. Athaliah's husband, Jehoram, was weak-willed and not a man of deep conviction. Although his forefathers had worshipped God, he allowed Athaliah to turn many of the Jews toward the worship of Baal, and he followed her, as well.

Once Athaliah tasted power during her husband's reign, she counseled her son in the ways of Baal after he inherited the throne. But when he was killed, Athaliah saw her chance to take power for herself by killing all others in line for the throne. However, her late husband's daughter hid one of Athaliah's grandsons for six years until his entitlement to the throne was revealed in public.

Athaliah was killed for her evil schemes. She never repented and never reconciled with God; the evil in her soul remained.

About Her

Athaliah was married to Jehoram (or Joram), King of Judah, the son of Jehoshaphat. Her father was Ahab, King of Israel, and her grandfather was King Omri. Her son, Ahaziah, inherited the throne of Judah when her husband died. And ultimately her grandson, Joash, reigned as King of Judah.

Apply Her

Any lost soul is an eternal tragedy; so we have to be careful who we follow and where we lead others. Proverbs 28:10 says, "Whoso causeth the righteous to go astray in an evil way, he shall fall himself into his own pit: but the upright shall have good things in possession." It is not just ignorance, but pure evil when, out of selfishness and rebellion against God, His people are led away from Him.

Find Her

2 Kings 8:16–27

2 Kings 11:1–21

2 Chronicles 21:1–7

2 Chronicles 22:2–3, 9–12

2 Chronicles 23:1–21

2 Chronicles 24:7

I AM

Queen Vashti

*To bring Vashti the queen before
the king with the crown royal, to
shew the people and the princes her
beauty: for she was fair to look on.*

Esther 1:11

I was once queen of Persia and married to King Ahasuerus. I was known as a woman of great beauty. But I didn't like the fact that my husband was always commanding me to do things. After all, he was not the boss of me. I was my own woman!

One day he called for me during a wild party that had gone on for days. I knew he was probably drunk, and I really didn't appreciate that he wanted me to parade my beauty before his guests. So, I refused. The king was more than angry. I guess I messed with his swagger a little too much; all the men at the party egged him on to put me in my place. They feared that if I got away with dissing my husband, all their women would start to dis- respect them. They decided my only worth was my beauty so he should get another, more beauti- ful queen. My husband listened to them and got rid of me.

What can I say? If my marriage was built only on my husband's opin- ion of my beauty, it was inevitable he would find a more beautiful woman, and my marriage would end. And that is exactly what happened; my husband found Esther and made her his queen.

Why Her?

Vashti and her husband, Ahasuerus, were pagans who worshipped all kinds of gods, but not the God of Israel. Ahasuerus was an immoral man—he may have had a queen, but he was not faithful to any woman. Vashti's position was always fragile because, since Ahasuerus didn't value women in general, he didn't value her. It does appear that he thought about her after she was banished. He may have even missed her until those closest to him suggested he find a new "young virgin," "a girl," not a woman to wed (Est. 2:1–4).

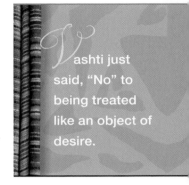

Vashti just said, "No" to being treated like an object of desire.

Vashti is seen by some to have been a cruel and evil woman—high and mighty, a woman who thought she was better than everyone else. So, when her husband summoned her from her banquet with the women of the court, she refused him. Others see her as an early feminist who refused to appear naked before her husband and his buddies who had been drinking for weeks. They see her act as one of high self-esteem—standing with pride despite what she knew would be dire consequences. They consider she just said, "No" to being treated like an object of desire.

Whichever story is true, Queen Vashti descended from worshippers of idols and destroyers of God's temple. It was

God's plan to remove Vashti from her royal position in order to elevate the one He had chosen for that position "for just such a time as this" (Est. 4:14). Israel had been captured by Vashti's grandfather, and it was time for God's people to be let go. It was Vashti's actions that made way for Esther to enact God's plan to bring about the days "wherein the Jews rested from their enemies, and the month which was turned unto them from sorrow to joy, and from mourning into a good day: that they should make them days of feasting and joy, and of sending portions one to another, and gifts to the poor" (Est. 9:22).

About Her

Vashti was the daughter of King Belshazzar of Babylon and the great-granddaughter of King Nebuchadnezzar, the man who destroyed the first Temple in Jerusalem. She was married to Ahasuerus, who succeeded Darius I as the King of Persia. Vashti had been captured by Darius I and presented to Ahasuerus as a suitable wife. Nothing is said about Ahasuerus picking Vashti for himself.

*I*srael had been captured by Vashti's grandfather, and it was time for God's people to be let go.

Apply Her

It is up to us to break off any negative traditions from our families. It is also up to us to surrender our lives to the Lord in order to be included in those He has predestined to affect the world around us, as did Esther (Rom. 8:29).

Vashti was merely a pawn to move out of the way because she served gods other than the one true God. Whom do you serve?

Find Her

Esther 1:9–22

Esther 2:1–4, 17

I AM

Esther

*For if thou altogether holdest thy
peace at this time, then shall there
enlargement and deliverance arise
to the Jews from another place; but
thou and thy father's house shall
be destroyed: and who knoweth
whether thou art come to the
kingdom for such a time as this?*

Esther 4:14

*M*y real name is Hadassah, but most people call me Esther. I was exiled from Jerusalem, and I lived as an outcast in a foreign land. Along with many other young ladies, I was taken to the palace, so the king could choose from among us those who would be part of his harem. Mordecai, my cousin who raised me, told me not to tell anyone of my Jewish heritage. We are so hated; it could have cost me my life.

The king picked me, of all the girls, to be his queen. What a comfortable life I expected! You can imagine how I reacted when Mordecai told me to approach the king and plead with him to save my people from the evil plan of revenge against the Jews put in motion by Haman. I feared approaching the king without invitation. The law says anyone who does so will be put to death.

But I had to stand up for my people. I had to have the faith and trust God's plan would work for my good and the good of others, even if I died in the process. After I fasted, I went to the king, and his eyes were opened to Haman's plot. The king did not order my death; instead, he ordered that Haman be hanged. The king signed an edict that saved the Jews from being killed and allowed them freedoms that caused joy and gladness among them. Just think, God used me, a girl born into nothing, to save an entire people.

Why Her?

Esther was an unlikely candidate to save her people. She was in exile, an outcast, and of a race hated by those in power. She was young and powerless, and then became a harem girl just struggling to stay alive. What a demonstration that God can change our circumstances in just one breath! He took this unknown, powerless orphan and raised her to a level of influence, second only to the king of Persia.

Esther's influence was not just a result of God's desire to bless her. There was greater purpose for God setting her in that place at that time. The Jewish people were targeted by an official in the king's court. God chose Esther and gave her the mission to save her people, but the mission put her life in danger. In that moment, Esther did not call out to God to alter her destiny or plead with Him to change what she must do; He was clearly present in the moment when she uttered the eternally significant words, "If I perish, I perish."

God was clearly present in the moment when Esther uttered the eternally significant words, "If I perish, I perish."

It was then that she surrendered everything to God and answered her calling. In doing so, she preserved God's plan that Jesus would arise out of the Jewish people. If she had not answered, God's plan would have been carried out without her, but she would have truly missed her purposed place of honor.

About Her

Esther, whose Hebrew name was Hadassah, was an orphan from the tribe of Benjamin. We don't know what happened to her parents, but she was adopted and raised by her cousin, Mordecai. Haman and Mordecai were destined to be mortal enemies because Haman was an Amalekite; his people had been enemies of Israel for centuries.

Apply Her

It is not up to us to set our own course in life. We must be ready to answer God's call and become the powerful women of God He created us to be.

Find Her

Esther 3:5–15
Esther 4

I AM

The Virtuous Woman

*Who can find a
virtuous woman?
For her price is far
above rubies.*

Proverbs 31:10

I'm not a real woman, but an ideal, a model. I am a picture of what a godly woman should be. Let's see: I always do good to my husband; I work industriously and willingly; I buy, prepare, and serve food to my household; I find ways to increase my family's provision; I am wise and kind and always give to the poor. For all my labors, I receive a great reward: my husband and my children call me blessed!

Some women are blessed to have people who love them and believe they live up to my standards. Others read my description and feel lacking and hopeless. Some mothers-in-law use the proverb about me like a laundry list describing the ideal daughter-in-law. But no woman should despair if her life isn't yet a copy of mine. Like the proverb says, "Who can find a virtuous woman?" It is enough that you want to be like me.

You are you, and that's a good thing. But God will work with you and in you so the qualities I possess will become your own. If you really want to be more like me, tell God the areas you would like to improve in, and work diligently with Him to achieve your goals. You may want to post my attributes on your refrigerator with a magnet as a reminder of your goals. Don't expect perfection; strive for daily progress and ever-growing maturity.

Why Her?

God wants us to have a picture of what we should strive for as women. The virtuous woman spoken of in Proverbs has all the attributes of a fully-functioning contributor. For too long, women have mistakenly thought their portrayal in the Bible was limited to just possessing a pretty face or being a kind of slave to their husbands. It may seem women are never portrayed as self-thinkers. Proverbs 31 shows the errors in those beliefs.

The woman represented in this final proverb is a woman who can do anything for her family and is a powerful force in her own right. Contained in these few verses is a long list of qualities a virtuous woman possesses, but none of them can apply unless she is first a woman who fears the Lord. If she does, she will be valued and praised by her husband, and her children will call her blessed.

The woman represented in this final proverb is a woman who can do anything for her family and is a powerful force in her own right.

About Her

The virtuous woman is a composite of the ideal woman—one a mother would want her son to marry. This proverb is a poem in which each verse starts with consecutive letters of the Hebrew alphabet.

Apply Her

In Christ, we can each be the virtuous woman who can do all things through Christ Jesus who strengthens us (Phil. 4:13). We should speak these verses over ourselves and embrace everything they say, claiming each quality as our own. God created us to be virtuous women and nothing can hold us back if we trust Him to enable us.

Find Her

Proverbs 31:10–31

I AM

The Shulamite Woman

Thou art all fair, my love;
there is no spot in thee.

Song of Solomon 4:7

I was a woman in love. It was amazing to love and be loved so generously. God meant for men and women to meet and be joined in love. This journey of love between a man and a woman is most delicious and delightful when it happens the way God planned it.

You see, my love courted me and wooed me and put me high on a pedestal, never taking from me, but always giving to me. Like you, I was black and beautiful (Song of Solomon 1:5); Solomon, my beloved, described me as "fairest among women" (Song of Solomon 1:8) and "my sister, my love, my dove, my undefiled" (Song of Solomon 5:2). See what I mean? That man's words and actions toward me got my head spinning.

I came to him as a virgin; so I knew no man but him. He was all I could ever want or dream of, and he did not disappoint. I was vulnerable, and he did not take advantage of me. I followed the direction of my people, waiting for a good man to find me and pursue me. This is God's way for a man to love a woman and a woman to love a man. It certainly worked for me.

Why Her?

We find the story of the Shulamite woman in the Song of Solomon. It is a beautiful story about honor, commitment, beauty, passion, and the pure satisfaction of love.

The Shulamite woman was a woman of very little means. She worked outside every day in the vineyards with her brothers. King Solomon chanced to see her as he was traveling and viewing his vineyards. He was taken by her beauty. He wooed her, won her heart, and asked her to be his bride. Though once a poor, vineyard worker, the Shulamite woman found herself on her way to becoming a queen.

Through this honest, intimate story, we see real love between a husband and wife. We see a woman who passionately loves her man and longs for him; she knows what she wants and goes after her love. This type of loves goes beyond the surface and dives deep into the soul and spirit.

About Her

The Shulamite woman was probably from an area in Issachar called Shunem (Joshua 19:18, 23).

Apply Her

Do you want to find the man God has for you? The Song of Solomon is a beautiful poem that reveals a perfect love. This is so because the Shulamite woman and her lover did things God's way in their courtship. It worked for them then, and it will work for you now. If you follow God's plan for a mate, you will never again be in danger of being taken advantage of or being used by the wrong man. God's way is fool-proof, but it also takes patience and faith.

The love revealed in the Song of Solomon can also be symbolic of God's love for His people. God's love for us is rich and deep. He is passionately in love with us no matter our place in life. Even though we are not perfect, we are made perfect through Him. He sees us as perfected through eyes of love, just as Solomon could see no flaws in the one He loved.

Find Her

Song of Solomon 1:4–6
Song of Solomon 6

I AM

Mary,

THE MOTHER OF JESUS

Now the birth of Jesus Christ was on this wise: When as his mother Mary was espoused to Joseph, before they came together, she was found with child of the Holy Ghost.

Matthew 1:18

ho am I that the Lord would bless me among women? You could say that I once was a young country bumpkin—a naïve virgin. I was looking forward to marrying my betrothed, Joseph. Then, one day, a commanding angel from God, named Gabriel, suddenly appeared. He told me not to be afraid because I had found great favor with God. What he told me was unbelievable, yet I knew it was true! I was to be the mother of the Messiah, the Son of God! Wow! But, as a virgin, I couldn't understand how such a thing could happen. The angel explained that the Holy Spirit would come upon me, and that is how I would conceive.

Then the angel told me my cousin, Elisabeth, was also pregnant. Me, a virgin, and she beyond childbearing years; yet both of us were to be living testimonies that nothing is impossible for God.

I couldn't wait to run to Elisabeth's house and tell her what I knew. But when I got there, it almost seemed she already knew. I felt so blessed that I was able to share such a miracle with her without her thinking me crazy. I stayed with her for the next three months and we were able to share with each other the unfolding of what God had spoken into each of our lives.

Why Her?

Why did God choose Mary to be Jesus' mother? Mary was no different from any one of us. She was not royalty, but an everyday person. If we know nothing else from Scripture, we know God selected everyday people to carry out extraordinary acts. All they needed to be used of God was a willing heart. Mary certainly had that.

When the angel, Gabriel, came to her and explained that God had favored her to be the mother of the "Son of the Highest" (Luke 1:32), she didn't know how such a thing could happen. But she immediately submitted herself saying, "Behold the handmaid of the Lord; be it unto me according to thy word" (Luke 1:38). Then she rushed off in excitement to go tell her cousin, Elisabeth.

From that time and throughout Jesus' life, Mary was by Jesus' side, nurturing Him, watching His ministry begin, travelling with Him to tend to His needs,

Behold the handmaid
of the Lord; be it unto me
according to thy word.
(Luke 1:38)

crying for Him in the darkest of hours, and rejoicing in His destiny fulfilled. She didn't always understand her Son or the complete calling on His life, but she knew who He was, that He was called to greatness, and that she was honored each day that God had allowed her to be His mother.

About Her

Mary was married to Joseph. Her father was Helis and her children were James, Joses, Simon, Judas, and Jesus, the Christ.

Apply Her

Do you call your children blessed and thank God every day that He blessed you to be their mother? That is your calling and who God made you to be. He put children in your hands who are destined for greatness in God's kingdom. He called you to nurture their growth, help them to know their own callings, tend to their needs, cry for them in the dark times, and rejoice with them as God reveals Himself in their lives. Every child is precious in God's sight, and you have been given a holy task of stewardship over the children placed in your care—whether in birth, in a classroom, in your neighborhood, or in your extended family.

Find Her

Isaiah 7:14

Matthew 1:16–25

Matthew 2:11

Matthew 27:55–61

Mark 6:3–4

Luke 1:26–56

Luke 2:4–35, 41–51

John 2:1–12

John 19:25, 26

Acts 1:13–14

I AM

The Canaanite Woman

Then Jesus answered and said unto her, O woman, great is thy faith: be it unto thee even as thou wilt. And her daughter was made whole from that very hour.

Matthew 15:28

*M*y daughter was full of demons and needed healing. I knew Jesus could cast them out; but I was a Gentile and Jesus seemed to only help the Jews. I had to go to Him anyway and beg Him to help me.

I went to Him and asked Him to have mercy on me. At first, He ignored me; so I went to His disciples and asked them to get Him to help me. When they asked, He said that He had enough to do just helping the Jews.

I was desperate for my daughter to be saved; so I knelt before Jesus on my knees and begged Him. Once again, He did not help me. This time, He said it was not right to take the food from the children and give it to the dogs. I had no pride left. I didn't care that I had been compared to a dog. I told Him even dogs like me need the left over scraps.

Then, Hallelujah! He told me He had healed my daughter right there and then, without Him being anywhere near her. I knew it was true. He said He healed her because I had great faith. The truth is that I knew who Jesus was, and I knew He was the only One who could help me.

Why Her?

In the story of the Canaanite woman, we see a mother who was willing to do whatever it took for her daughter to be healed. She had a desperate need and knew Jesus was the only one who could help her.

Knowing she might be rejected because she was a woman and a Gentile, she took a chance and cried out, "Have mercy on me, O Lord, thou son of David; my daughter is grievously vexed with a devil" (Matt. 15:22). When she did not receive an answer the first time, she continued to ask. Even when it seemed Jesus would not answer her, she kept asking. She believed because of who He was that He would eventually answer her pleas. She followed Jesus and cried out to Him to heal her daughter. The disciples wanted Jesus to send her away; but Jesus saw her great faith. The Canaanite woman was persistent; she was driven by faith and love. Even when He appeared to answer her, but did

Have mercy on me, O Lord, thou son of David; my daughter is grievously vexed with a devil. (Matt. 15:22)

not grant her petition, still she persisted. She believed Jesus would answer her cry for help and respond with love for her daughter.

About Her

The Canaanite woman is not named; but she is Greek, a Syrophenician, living in the Tyre-Sidon area of Canaan.

Apply Her

We can always trust in God's love and mercy—even when it seems our requests are not immediately answered. God honors the faith we have in Him, no matter who we are. He can look straight into our hearts and see whether we are truly desperate for Him.

Find Her

Matthew 15:21–28

Mark 7:25–30

I AM

Salome,

WIFE OF ZEBEDEE

*And many women were there
beholding afar off, which followed
Jesus from Galilee, ministering
unto him: Among which was
Mary Magdalene, and Mary the
mother of James and Joses, and
the mother of Zebedees children.*

Matthew 27:55–56

*M*y sons, James and John, were two of Jesus' disciples. Along with my sons, my husband, Zebedee, and I were followers of Jesus.

I was so proud of my sons. I wanted them to have a place of honor in the kingdom of God. I took it upon myself to obtain a favorable position for them; I asked Jesus to let one of my sons sit on His left side and the other on His right side in His kingdom.

But Jesus said I didn't know what I was asking and what would be required of those who held those places of honor. I knew my boys could do whatever was asked of them; but Jesus went on to say that those positions were not His to give. He told me only God the Father could determine who sat in those places of honor by His side.

I was disappointed, but our family continued to serve the Lord with all our might. Even as He was crucified, I longed to minister to Him and care for Him. I was there, watching as they did such horrible things to my Lord; yet nothing shook my faith in Him, and I honored His sacrifice by giving my whole life to Him.

Why Her?

Salome stands in the background and encourages her husband and sons to be all God called them to be. But what about her? What was her calling?

Salome was a strong woman of faith who wanted her family to know God; but more importantly, she wanted Him to know them. Her calling was to be her husband's helpmate and to nurture, prepare, position, and propel her sons as they became two of Jesus' twelve disciples. Some would say her sons' callings had nothing to do with hers, but they would be wrong. Throughout the Bible, God called many women to be "stage mothers" to their children because they were charged with protecting the calling of God on their children's lives; these mothers were a kind of early childhood body guard. Salome is best known for stepping up to Jesus and making a case with Him to give her sons a place of honor in heaven. Yes, she was bold; and whether she crossed the line with her questioning of Jesus or not, Jesus knew she acted out of real love for her sons.

She, her husband, and her two sons—James and John—called Jesus their friend; and they remained His friends throughout His ministry. Salome is one of the women who travelled with Jesus and took care of Him. She also witnessed both Jesus' crucifixion and Jesus' empty tomb. Her reward was to know that, as a woman of faith, she would get to spend eternity with her family in the presence of God.

About Her

Salome is the wife of Zebedee and the mother of James and John, Jesus' disciples. It is also believed that she is Jesus' mother, Mary's sister and Jesus' aunt." This insertion is necessary because I say for Mary Magdalene that she was the only woman who witnessed the crucifixion that was not related to Jesus.

Apply Her

All of us are called to selflessness in the kingdom of God. But as mothers, whether we work outside the home or not, one of our greatest callings is to sacrifice ourselves for the benefit of our children. We are to be imparters of Jesus Christ into every aspect of our children's lives and to protect the calling of God upon them.

Since God has given you stewardship over your children's lives, this should be your first priority outside of your relationship with the Lord and your oneness with your husband. Do not let busyness and the distractions of the modern world cause you to miss this important call on your life.

Find Her

Matthew 20:20–22

Matthew 27:50–56

Mark 16:1–8

Luke 8:1–3

Luke 24:1–11

I AM

The Woman

WITH THE ISSUE OF BLOOD

*And if a woman have an issue
of her blood many days out of
the time of her separation, or
if it run beyond the time of her
separation she shall be unclean.*

Leviticus 15:25

I had been bleeding for twelve years! It was a terrible burden to live that way. The Law of God says that as long as a woman has an issue of blood, she is to be separated from everyone else because she is unclean. This means that if she touches anyone else, they will also be unclean.

I was lonely and set apart from my family. And I was penniless because I had spent all my money on doctors, none of whom could find a cure. But, I knew if I could just get to Jesus, He could heal me. A crowd surrounded Him that day, so I pushed my way through and touched just the hem of His robe. Instantly, I knew my bleeding had ended. Jesus stopped and asked, "Who touched me?" He knew power had gone from Him.

I was so afraid. I had thought He wouldn't notice me because I was just part of the crowd—only one of many who had touched Him. I was the unclean one, though He didn't seem concerned with that fact. Trembling, I confessed immediately. He told me not to worry and to go in peace because my faith had healed me. That I did, thankful that my Lord did not turn from my unclean state. All that mattered to Him was my faith in Him.

Why Her?

Jesus' encounter with the Woman with the Issue of Blood happened as the result of Jesus' detour on His way to respond to Jarius' request for Jesus to heal his daughter.

The woman who had been ill for twelve years was viewed by everyone, including herself, as less than nothing. She was a total outcast who had been unclean for over a decade, which means she was not permitted to associate with anyone or touch anyone, let alone let anyone touch her. She was not even allowed to participate in religious activities; yet, she knew Jesus and had faith. Even though she hoped beyond hope that just touching Jesus' hem would heal her, she probably fully expected that she was in serious trouble when He asked who had touched Him. But Jesus knew her and loved her, respected her and valued her, when no one else would or could. At the moment she reached out to Jesus, no one was more important to Him than she. Nothing diverted His attention from her.

The woman who had been ill for twelve years was viewed by everyone, including herself, as less than nothing.

About Her

Little is known about the Woman with the Issue of Blood, but the incident reported occurred in A.D. 26–30, near the Sea of Galilee.

Apply Her

Whenever we feel broken and like outcasts, like no one truly loves or cares, we need only draw near to Jesus and reach out to touch the hem of His garment. He will love us, respect us, value us, and heal us, just as He did this Woman with the Issue of Blood.

Find Her

Mark 5:22–34

I AM
Elisabeth

And they had no child, because that Elisabeth was barren, and they both were now well stricken in years.

Luke 1:7

I had faith in God and kept His commandments and ordinances. I tried to live a blameless life before Him—even when, for many years, God did not see fit to bless my husband, Zacharias, and me with children. But when I was long past menopause and had suffered all the indignities that can be heaped upon a barren woman, I became pregnant. The mighty angel, Gabriel, appeared before my husband and foretold our son's birth; he is a blessing from God. Zacharias made the mistake of questioning the possibility, and Gabriel struck him mute until our son was born.

I never doubted for a moment that what the angel said was true. I prepared for the birth of my son, who was to be named John, as the angel had instructed us. When my young cousin, Mary, came to my home, the baby leapt inside of me just upon hearing her voice. I knew then that she was to be the mother of our Lord, and she knew in her spirit the wonder that was foretold for me.

The Holy Spirit allowed us to confirm to one another the Word from the Lord that was given to each of us. It was nice to have someone with whom to share the amazing news. So Mary stayed with me for three months until John was born. After his birth, everyone knew I was not cursed by the Lord, but had found favor in His eyes. Mary and I now share a special bond because we were able to share God's miracle-working Word.

Why Her?

It was a big thing for Elisabeth and her husband, Zacharias to be called "blameless" before God. Zacharias was of the priesthood, and he and Elisabeth had both dedicated their lives to the faith; they lived righteous lives before God. God honored them in their old age by answering their long-time, silent prayer—He sent them a child. This special child would carry with him a mighty purpose for the kingdom of God. A child such as this needed parents who possessed great faith. After all, how could a child in the womb be filled with the Holy Spirit if his mother was not?

God had very specific instructions on how Elisabeth's and Zacharias' son, John, was to be raised. It was necessary that his parents hear God clearly, so there was no doubt about those instructions. Elisabeth was to be the mother of "one crying in the wilderness"—the one who would announce the coming of Jesus Christ. To be his mother was both a kingdom honor and an awesome responsibility—one that Elisabeth was fully equipped to take on. Just

God had very specific instructions on how Elisabeth's and Zacharias' son, John, was to be raised.

as her son would announce the Messiah's coming, Elisabeth would confirm the revelation given to her younger cousin, Mary. Elisabeth knew in her spirit that Mary would be blessed among women to be the mother of the Messiah.

About Her

Elisabeth was a descendant of Aaron and the wife of Zacharias. Her cousin was Mary, Jesus' mother.

Apply Her

Elisabeth thought her usefulness was coming to an end as she served God beside her husband for many long years. But, to God, her steadfast faith was reason enough to call Elisabeth into a new assignment.

For as long as God gives us each the breath of life, we must give that life back to Him—dedicated to His service and the fulfillment of His purposes. In the kingdom of God there is no such thing as too old.

Find Her

Luke 1:5-7, 24–25, 36–45, 57–60

I AM

Anna

And there was one Anna, a prophetess, the daughter of Phanuel, of the tribe of Aser: she was of a great age, and had lived with an husband seven years from her virginity.

Luke 2:36

I was very young when my husband died. I was devastated, particularly since I had no children. But I am a woman of faith, so I dedicated my life to God. Day and night, I prayed and fasted in the temple as I waited for the coming of the Messiah. As the faithful came into the temple, I would also pray over them and prophesy.

I prayed that God would allow me to live long enough to see our Savior come into this world. I watched and waited more than eighty years, for I knew that the Holy One was coming.

When Mary and Joseph brought their baby into the temple, I knew right away who He was. The blessed Redeemer had arrived to take away the sin of the world. I blessed the Lord for Him and then departed from the temple and went back to Nazareth. My prayers and the prayers of the world had been answered. I praise God for the Lord Jesus Christ, who is the Savior of us all.

Why Her?

Anna was a blessed woman indeed. She had the unique honor of being in the presence of the infant Jesus and knowing who He was and why He had come into the world. But it was no accident that Anna was chosen by God to be introduced to His only Son.

After Anna's husband died only seven years after their marriage (presumably when she was young), Anna devoted herself to God and never left the temple. She had no life apart from Him. She fasted and prayed without ceasing and prayed over those who came into the temple. (There are some things that only happen with fasting and praying.) Anna set herself apart with her steadfast faith that God would show up in that place, and He did literally! What a prayer this woman prayed! She asked that God would let her live long enough to see the Savior come into the world! God heard her prayer, saw her heart for Him, and gave her what her heart desired.

Anna set herself apart with her steadfast faith that God would show up in that place and He did literally!

About Her

Anna was a widow most of her long life and the daughter of Phanuel from the tribe of Aser, which had turned from idols and come back to God.

Apply Her

When we surrender our lives to God, He will reveal Himself by bringing us face-to-face with His Son, Jesus, Lord of all. He will deposit in our hearts great desires that He will delight in giving us.

Find Her

Luke 2:36–38

I AM

Mary Magdalene

*And certain women, which had
been healed of evil spirits and
infirmities, Mary called Magdalene,
out of whom went seven devils,
and Joanna the wife of Chuza
Herod's steward, and Susanna,
and many others, which ministered
unto him of their substance.*

Luke 8:2–3

I owe Jesus my whole life. He saved me in so many ways. When He met me, I was deep in sin and full of demons. He cast seven demons out of me and gave me peace. After that, I surrendered my life to Him and called Him Lord. I followed Jesus even to the foot of the cross.

Although I knew it would be unbearable, I had to be at the crucifixion and witness what happened. It was hideous beyond words! But I knew then, more than ever, that He was exactly who He claimed to be: the Son of Man and Son of God.

As I cared for Him in His life, I helped tend to Him in His death. I visited His tomb early one morning to anoint His body; but when I got there, His body was gone! I was beside myself with grief; but an angel of the Lord came to me and told me Jesus had risen from the dead!

Then I saw Him myself. At first I didn't recognize Him; but when He called my name, I knew Him at once. I had spent so much time with Jesus that when I heard His voice, I recognized it right away and I answered him: "Master!"

Why Her?

The story of Mary Magdalene is a story about friendship and servanthood. Before she met Jesus, Mary was full of demons and sickness, which made her unclean and unfit to be in decent company. Jesus didn't care what man thought of her. God had created her individually and on purpose, and He was not about to give up on her. Jesus cured her of everything, and in return, she became His devoted follower and one of several women who travelled with Him and the apostles. Along with the other women, she helped them and took care of them. It may not have seemed particularly appropriate for a single woman to be traveling with a group of men, but she didn't care what people thought. She lived only to serve God. As a result, she became one of Jesus' most beloved friends and followers.

Mary Magdalene was the only woman at the cross who was not a member of Jesus' family. She witnessed His burial, and was the first to see the resurrected Jesus.

Mary Magdalene was the only woman at the cross who was not a member of Jesus' family.

About Her

Mary is from Magdalena, which is why she is called Mary Magdalene. She is identified by her hometown because she had no husband to identify her.

Apply Her

Even when the whole world gives up on us, none of us is ever a lost cause to Jesus. If we seek Him with all our hearts, we will find Him. Even if our lives are so tangled and knotted that it seems nothing can undo all the craziness, God will take our lives, no matter how big the mess. What He will give back are abundant lives full of purpose and meaning (John 10:10).

Find Her

Luke 8:1–3
Luke 23:49–56
Luke 24:10–11
John 19:25
John 20:1–18

I AM
Martha

And Jesus answered and said unto her, Martha, Martha, thou art careful and troubled about many things.

Luke 10:41

I was beside myself! Jesus was coming to our house to teach. He is our Lord, and my house needed to be cleaned from top to bottom. I wondered what I could possibly serve the One who does miracles. There was so much to do as the people arrived: making drinks, bringing food, and making everyone comfortable.

I couldn't understand my sister, Mary. She was doing nothing to help me. She was acting like a guest and just sitting down at Jesus' feet. Couldn't she see I needed help in the kitchen?

I finally had had enough! Jesus didn't seem to notice she wasn't helping me, and He said nothing to her. So, I asked Him why. I felt so foolish when He cautioned me that rushing around was causing me to miss the purposes for which He had come. I was missing His teaching because of my busyness. I realized that, at times, I should be like my sister and just sit at His feet.

I learned my lesson well, and I've tried to stay focused on my faith. When my brother, Lazarus, died before Jesus could get to him, I still believed that God could and would do all things through Jesus, who is the Messiah. I believed it was not too late for Jesus to save my brother. My faith did not return void— Jesus raised my brother from the dead!

Why Her?

Martha was the responsible one. She was the one who made sure things were in order. She made sure Jesus was honored when He came to her home. She believed honoring Him meant the house must be clean, the food must be cooked, and the people must be served. There was so much she carried on her shoulders.

Martha represents the busyness of this world which can distract us from spending time with God. She had Jesus right in front of her; she was in His presence! But all she could see was serving and cleaning. When she complained that Mary was not doing her part, Jesus spoke to her and let her know that spending time with Him was honoring Him. Once she realized she couldn't impress Him with superficial things, she learned to come to Jesus just as she was. She realized He only wanted her heart.

Martha represents the busyness of this world which can distract us from spending time with God.

About Her

Martha is the sister of Mary and Lazarus. She lived in the town of Bethany.

Apply Her

Even when we are about the Master's work, we have to take personal time to meet with Him and not let the external trappings keep us from saturating ourselves in the presence of God.

Find Her

Luke 10:38–42
John 11:1–44
John 12:1–2

I AM

Mary,

SISTER OF LAZARUS

Then took Mary a pound of
ointment of spikenard, very costly,
and anointed the feet of Jesus,
and wiped his feet with her hair:
and the house was filled with
the odour of the ointment.

John 12:3

I wish my sister, Martha, would just sit down somewhere. She's always busy, always doing something. But she's missing everything! She even allowed her busyness to pull her from Jesus when He was teaching here in our home. That was not the time to be cleaning and feeding people.

Well, I stayed right at Jesus' feet, as close as I could get. As a woman, men won't teach me the ways of God; but Jesus was not afraid of man's opinion. He taught anyone who would listen, even women.

But when my brother, Lazarus, fell ill, it was four days before Jesus got here and Lazarus died. I thought it was too late. I did not believe anyone could raise the dead. So, I didn't even go out to meet Jesus when He arrived. Then I saw His power with my own eyes. We all stood and watched as, at Jesus' command, my brother arose from the dead and walked out of His tomb!

My view of the Lord changed that day; instead of seeing Jesus just as my teacher, I then understood that He is my Savior. The next time He came to dinner, I honored Him by massaging His feet with the expensive oils I had been saving; then I dried them with my hair. I gave Jesus the best I had to give.

Why Her?

In Mary's day it was no everyday thing for women to have the opportunity to be in the presence of a great teacher. And she didn't waste one minute of her opportunity to be in the presence of the Master. She not only had the honor of calling Jesus her Lord, but also of calling Him a personal friend. When He spoke, she listened, hanging on to every word. When He spoke, the dishes could wait and so could the company.

So how is it that, when Lazarus fell ill and died, Mary did not understand Jesus could raise him from the dead? Mary believed Jesus is Lord and that "whatsoever thou wilt ask of God, God will give it thee" (John 11:22). However, she still could not grasp all that Jesus was capable of doing. But once Jesus revealed that part of Himself to her, she believed.

Mary believed Jesus is Lord and that "whatsoever thou wilt ask of God, God will give it thee." (John 11:22)

About Her

Mary is the sister of Martha and Lazarus and lived in the town of Bethany

Apply Her

Getting to know Jesus is a slow roll and not an all-of-a sudden thing. He reveals Himself to us little by little, unfolding the mystery of who He is (1 Cor.13:12) until we come face to face with Him.

Find Her

Luke 10:38–42
John 11:1–44
John 12:1–2

I AM

The Samaritan Woman

But whosoever drinketh of the water
that I shall give him shall never
thirst; but the water that I shall give
him shall be in him a well of water
springing up into everlasting life.

John 4:14

195

One seemingly normal day, I walked down to the well to fetch some water. I came upon a man there who asked me to bring Him a drink from the well. I was shocked! The man was clearly a Jew, and I was a Samaritan. The Jews considered us nothing more than dirt. But this man spoke strange words about His identity and the living waters He could bring to my thirsty soul. He said drinking the water from the well would only leave me thirsting again; but He promised if I would drink from His living water, I would have everlasting life.

Then He asked me to go get my husband and I told Him I didn't have one. He responded by telling me about all the men in my past. He knew the man I lived with was not my husband. I realized He was a prophet.

He spoke of salvation; He told me it was not just for the Jews; it was for everyone, even me! I had heard about the promised Messiah who would come into the world and answer all my questions; I wondered if the man before me could be the One. I told everyone about Him. Many came to hear what He had to say and left believing as I did, that truly, He is the Son of God.

Why Her?

The Samaritan woman was considered to be socially and spiritually of less value than any man—first, she was a woman and, therefore, held a place of subservience in these ancient days; second, she was a Samaritan. Samaritans had a history of being hated and avoided by the Jews, so this Samaritan woman was an unlikely student of the Jewish teacher, as Jesus was called. But Jesus, the Savior, went out of His way to come through Samaria just to meet with this woman. We know that it was a divine appointment because Jews avoided Samaria in their travels because they considered Samaritans to be ungodly and unclean; but Jesus purposefully chose this longer route between Judea and Galilee.

Drawing water was normally an activity reserved for cooler parts of the day. Though we cannot be sure why this woman chose to visit the well in the heat of the noonday sun, many assume it was because she suffered the lot of an outcast. Regardless of the reason behind her timing, we can be sure it was no accident that Jesus met her there.

The exchange between the Samaritan woman and Jesus is a sweet passage that is reminiscent of how each of us in our everyday lives, doing our everyday things, comes to meet with the Savior. Just as He approached this woman with humility and full acceptance, He approaches each of us gently and reveals Himself to us speaking words of truth, encouragement, and life to all who will listen. Though we may not recognize Him at first, He knows more about us than we know about ourselves. He knows where we are, where we have been, and where we will be; and He loves us through it all! Just as He seemed to invite the Samaritan woman's bold, probing questions, so He will always encourage us to seek His kingdom and obtain His truth. Just as she dropped her precious water jug and ran to tell what she had heard and seen, when we have seen and known the Lord nothing else should matter.

About Her

Samaritans were descendants of the tribes of Israel who had been conquered by Assyria. They intermarried and worshipped pagan idols as well as the God of Israel. Because of their adoption of idolatry, they were hated by the Jews; but Samaritans were some of the first to hear and accept the gospel of Jesus Christ.

Apply Her

Jesus wants each of us, no matter who we are, to thirst after Him. He wants us to know Him and then share the truth of His identity so others might also find Him and believe.

Find Her

John 4

I AM
Sapphira

Neither was there any among them
that lacked: for as many as were
possessors of lands or houses sold
them, and brought the prices of the
things that were sold, And laid
them down at the apostles' feet: and
distribution was made unto every
man according as he had need.

Act 4:34–35

I am Sapphira, wife of Ananias. As many in the church were doing, we sold some property, put a little away for a rainy day, and laid the rest at the apostles' feet. Okay, so we kept back a little. What is wrong with that? We might have stretched the truth when we claimed we were giving them all of it, but we just wanted to look good in front of the other saintly acting people. It really wasn't necessary for Peter to call my husband out on it. Especially since my husband died right there on the spot, probably out of sheer embarrassment. Later, when I arrived at the gathering where Peter was, he tricked me by asking me how much we got for the property. I did just what Ananias did—I lied. Peter also called me out about it; and I, too, gave up the ghost right there.

God made an example of Ananias and me. It's imperative to be honest, not deceitful, in our dealings. We paid a dear price for that lesson—the cost was our lives

Why Her?

Sapphira and her husband conspired to lie about the money they were donating to the apostles to be used in ministry. They didn't have to sell the property and give it all to the ministry; but once they said that was what they were doing, they were under an obligation to do what they said.

It is important to view this story in the context of the previous chapter, which explains how powerful the early church was and that they were of "one heart and one soul" (Acts 4:32). They saw their possessions as communal; and when they sold land, "they brought the prices of the things that were sold" as an offering (Acts 4:34). An example is given of Barnabas selling his land and laying all the proceeds at the apostles' feet (Acts 4:37). Well, that didn't happen with Sapphira and her husband; maybe they were pretending to be one with the others but were really just thinking selfishly. These co-conspirators must have thought their little lie didn't matter.

The most interesting part of this story, however, is that those around Ananias and Sapphira who witnessed

Sapphira and her husband conspired to lie about the money they were donating to the apostles to be used in ministry.

the scene had "great fear." But why should they have been scared when Sapphira and her husband died only because they lied? The people around them were probably convicted because many of them had told what they thought were insignificant, little, white lies. They may have thought, "so what?" But when Sapphira and her husband paid the price for their lie, the ones around them most likely realized any of them could have been buried that day, as well.

About Her

All we know about Sapphira is that she and her husband, Ananias, were members of the early Christian church.

Apply Her

To God, every lie is significant. Even when we think it doesn't matter much, or that we had good reasons for lying, it is sinful before God. He calls us to be truth-tellers and that means we cannot give ourselves a pass on even the smallest of untruths.

Find Her

Acts 4:31–37
Acts 5:1–11

I AM
Candace

*And he arose and went: and, behold,
a man of Ethiopia, an eunuch of
great authority under Candace queen
of the Ethiopians, who had the
charge of all her treasure, and had
come to Jerusalem for to worship,
was returning, and sitting in his
chariot read Esaias the prophet.*

Acts 8:27–28

I didn't know who Jesus was, but I knew someone who did. There was a man, high in my service, who had been baptized by water and was a strong believer in Jesus. I allowed this man to go to Jerusalem to worship his God. When he came back, he spread a new gospel and I allowed it. I may even have believed it myself. I thought everyone should hear this good news. After my servant's return it was not long until belief in the good news he shared spread throughout Ethiopia. Many in this nation became strong followers of Jesus Christ.

The Candace referred to in Acts 8:26–40 was a rich and powerful ruler.

Why Her?

Throughout history, particularly in the days of the Bible, it has usually been men who have ruled nations. However, Ethiopia was far ahead of its time. When the book of Acts was written, a line of queens ruled the African nation; these queens were known collectively as Candace.

The Candace referred to in Acts 8:26–40 was a rich and powerful ruler. In her benevolence, she had allowed her treasurer to travel to Jerusalem to worship. The devoted worshipper had traveled nearly 1,600 miles to worship in the holy city. The journey would have taken this devout man nearly a month.

Through a series of God-ordained events, this Ethiopian official was baptized by Philip, the evangelist, and it is believed he became the first gentile convert. His salvation marked the beginning of a fulfillment of the prophecy of David that says; "Ethiopia will quickly stretch out her hands to God" (Ps. 68:31).

The Ethiopian treasurer took the gospel back to Ethiopia and may have provided the seed for Christianity to grow in that nation, which, even now, has one of the largest Christian populations of any African nation.

The Candace of Acts was appointed to be queen at that time for a divine purpose. Because of her, Ethiopia had the opportunity to hear and embrace the gospel of Jesus Christ.

About Her

She was Queen of Ethiopia at the time of the Apostles. "Candace" was a name given to all Ethiopian Queens, like the use of "Pharaoh" in Egypt for kings.

Apply Her

We are all destined for greatness, however that greatness may appear. It is important to be in the positions God has for us. We never know how God may use our positions in life to have an impact on our world.

Find Her

Acts 8:26–28

I AM
Tabitha

*Now there was at Joppa a certain
disciple named Tabitha, which by
interpretation is called Dorcas:
this woman was full of good works
and alms deeds which she did.*

Acts 9:36

*M*y name is Tabitha. I was obedient to Jesus' command to love and serve others. But as I ministered in His name, I became very ill. Many with whom I served and many to whom I had ministered gathered around to pray for me. Yet, I died.

I am told several men, knowing Peter was in the vicinity, went to get him. Many people wondered why they would call Peter to the side of a dead woman. Others wondered if Peter would come.

Amazingly, Peter did come to Joppa. Those who had known me showed him some of my handiwork and told of my good deeds. Peter sent everyone away and kneeled down beside me and prayed. He called my name, saying, "Tabitha, arise." Praise, Jesus! I opened my eyes, saw Peter, and sat up. I had returned to life!

The people of Joppa went out and told the story of what had happened. Many of those who heard about the miracle of my resurrection believed and were saved.

You see, God saved me by raising me from the dead, but I already knew salvation. I served the Lord, and my calling was to use my life as a beacon to others—a light to their path to follow Jesus and be saved. God used my death and resurrection to save many.

Why Her?

Tabitha was a role model for the women of her time; she is also a model for us. She was most likely a widow who used what she had to help others. She was also known for her gentle ways and for making clothing for the poor. But she didn't do good works, so she could put it on her resumé or feel good about herself; her good works came from a heart full of faith. In fact, she is the only woman called a disciple in Scripture. Her motivation was to love and obey God and to love His people. In the process, she found joy in giving of her money, her time, and her talents.

Surely, God looked at Tabitha and found her a willing vessel. And He used her to demonstrate who He is through the supernatural powers He bestowed upon the Apostle Peter to raise her from the dead. What better proof to non-believers that God is real? What better show of His affection to Tabitha than to return life to her dead body. Only Jesus and His beloved friend, Lazarus, had been raised before. Now, through Tabitha's story, all can see that they,

Surely, God looked at Tabitha and found her a willing vessel. And He used her to demonstrate who He is.

too, can know resurrection life if they exercise their faith through Christ.

About Her

We know nothing about Tabitha's lineage except that she lived in Joppa. We also know her name means "gazelle" or "doe," which personifies a beautiful and gentle person.

Apply Her

Faith should not be something we just talk about. Faith is something we have to live out. It is a word that requires action when matched with what we believe. What good is it for us to believe in taking care of the poor and shut-ins and then not do it? What good is it for us to say that Christ lives in us and then complain about the life we have? What good is it for us to say that we trust God and then refuse to allow Him to change us?

Find Her

Acts 9:36–42

I AM

Eunice

When I call to remembrance the unfeigned faith that is in thee, which dwelt first in thy grandmother Lois, and thy mother Eunice; and I am persuaded that in thee also.

2 Timothy 1:5

I am Eunice, mother of Timothy. No mother could be prouder of her son. Although Timothy's father was Greek and would not allow Timothy to be circumcised as the Jewish faith demands, my son seemed to have been born with a spiritual hunger. Thankfully, Paul took Timothy under his wing and showed him how to be a man of God.

I take some credit as well. From the Proverbs, I knew if I raised Timothy in the ways of the Lord, he would not depart from those teachings when he grew older. From the very beginning I taught him the Scriptures and the ways of God.

My mother, Lois, was also instrumental in Timothy's spiritual growth. After all, she is the reason I learned to love the Lord. Do you see how this culture of Christ is passed from generation to generation? By watching your life and hearing the Scriptures, your children fall in love with the Lord. Then, through their faith and through diligent teaching of the Word, their children also fall in love with Him.

Our Timothy has taken his faith to new heights. He has become an example to many; he is wise in the Lord far beyond his years. Paul has encouraged him in his pastoral ministry despite his young age.

Why Her?

Eunice was Timothy's mother. She was a Greek raised as a Jew. She practiced her faith as she was taught by her mother, Lois. When she and her mother heard the words of Paul, they became followers of Jesus Christ. It is not clear how Eunice came to be unequally yoked with Timothy's father who was Greek and worshipped the Greek gods, but Eunice was well acquainted with the gospel and became the spiritual head of her family. At the same time she instructed Timothy, she made sure he was brought up in the faith and was surrounded by strong men of God, like Paul, who could be an example to him.

But Paul became more than an example. Paul treated Timothy like a son. Timothy surpassed Eunice's expectations and became the leader of the church at Ephesus at an age younger than most leaders. Paul took Timothy under his wing and taught him to lead with confidence. Even in Paul's last days, he fondly remembered the sincere faith of Eunice and her mother Lois.

Eunice was well acquainted with the gospel and became the spiritual head of her family.

About Her

Eunice was married to a Greek man who worshipped Greek gods. She lived in Lystra and was the daughter of Lois. She was the mother of Timothy, who led the church at Ephesus.

Apply Her

If we have children, we must start training them in the way they should go in the Lord as soon as they are born. If we have husbands who are not men of faith, we will have to step into that role of leading our children into lives of faith. Even before they can walk and talk and understand words, our children can understand the praises and worship we give to the Lord in their presence. We must teach them His ways so that when they are old, they will not depart from them (Prov. 22:6).

Find Her

Acts 16:1–3
2 Timothy 1:5

I AM

Lydia

And a certain woman named Lydia,
a seller of purple, of the city of
Thyatira, which worshipped God,
heard us: whose heart the Lord
opened, that she attended unto the
things which were spoken of Paul.

Acts 16:14

I am Lydia, a dealer in purple dyes and a straight-up business woman. I do okay with my business, and it gives me the freedom and flexibility to do what I need to do. There are so many things of this world my wealth would allow me to chase, but my passion is to worship the God of Israel and follow hard after His Son.

I loved God and made it a practice to worship Him regularly. On Sabbath days, I met with others by the river to worship Him. One day, Paul came to our meeting and told us about Jesus. As I listened to Paul, I came to a deep belief in Jesus the Messiah. I determined then and there to diligently seek God and learn about life in His kingdom. I was so thrilled when Paul and those with him agreed to stay at my home. God blessed me and my household abundantly. All of us gave our lives to the Lord and were baptized by Paul. We now serve the Lord together, but I am hungry to know more about the abundant life Jesus brings.

I have a busy schedule, and it is a blessing, but I have learned that I cannot let my daily hustle distract me from what is most important in life.

Why Her?

Lydia was a business woman who dealt in purple cloth. At that time purple was the color worn by royalty, and it was made by using shells from the ocean.

Lydia already loved God and was full of faith when she first heard Paul speak. Right away, she accepted Paul's teachings about the good news of Jesus. Lydia was a sold-out Christian whose actions spoke much louder than her words. She did not just sit still; she got baptized and began to put her faith into action.

First, Lydia made sure her entire household heard the good news of Jesus Christ and they all got baptized, as well. She was a busy woman, but she knew her priorities. She tracked down Paul and his followers and persuaded them to stay at her house. She was anxious to get more instruction and to serve them in any way she could.

Lydia made sure her entire household heard the good news of Jesus Christ and they all got baptized.

About Her

Lydia lived in the city of Thyatira. It is thought that her name indicates she comes from Lydia, the providence in which Thyatira is located. No mention is made of any family of Lydia, and she appeared to not be married.

Apply Her

Faith is not a passive word; it is an action word. Like Lydia we must get up and tell others the good news we have heard. Then we must serve the body of Christ with our time and resources.

Find Her

Acts 16:14–15

I AM
Apphia

*Paul, a prisoner of Jesus Christ, and
Timothy our brother, unto Philemon
our dearly beloved, and fellow
labourer, and to our beloved Apphia,
and Archippus our fellowsoldier,
and to the church in thy house.*

Philemon 1–2

*M*y husband, Philemon, and I were among the seventy apostles whom Jesus sent out with the twelve to spread the good news of the gospel. We had the honor of being baptized by Paul, and my husband was discipled by him. Philemon and I lived to honor Jesus and the good news He brought—so much so, our church met in our home.

We were rather wealthy, but we learned from Paul that our wealth was to be used for ministry. He taught us that we were to view all Christians, including slaves, as our brothers and sisters.

During Nero's reign the pagans celebrated regularly. At these times my husband and I met with a small group in our home to pray and honor God. When the pagans heard about what we were doing, they dragged us out of our home and stoned us until we gave up our spirits to God.

I was honored to serve in ministry next to my husband and to live and die only to know Jesus and make Him known.

Why Her?

Apphia was a co-laborer with her husband, Philemon, and their son Archippus, who was a pastor (see Col. 4:17). They opened their home and held Christian meetings there. They were bold Christians who put their lives on the line just to worship God.

It is no small thing that Apphia was called beloved. That one word evokes the understanding that she was sister, friend, gentle lady, and servant, all in one. In those days Christians were persecuted and alienated from their blood families. All they had was their family in Christ with whom they trusted their very lives.

In the end Apphia, Philemon, and Archippus were stoned to death for their faith. Apphia did not shy away from battling on the front lines with her husband and their son. They gave their lives in order to gain their lives.

Apphia was sister, friend, gentle lady, and servant, all in one.

About Her

Apphia is one of the only women counted by many as an apostle chosen by Jesus. She is the wife of Philemon, also an apostle. She lived during a time when being a Christian was not for the faint of heart. Nero had orchestrated the burning of Rome that devastated the city. When there was a rumored backlash from the people, Nero blamed the Christians for the blaze and ordered that they all die for this crime (and many other heinous acts of which he falsely accused them).

Christians in the early church put their lives on the line every day to practice their faith. If they were arrested, they were not just killed; they were put to death in the worst ways imaginable.

Apply Her

We may not currently face the kind of persecution that Apphia and her family faced; but we are called to die daily in the practice of our faith. This means we give up our lives and surrender them to Christ, living only for Him.

Find Her

Philemon 1–3

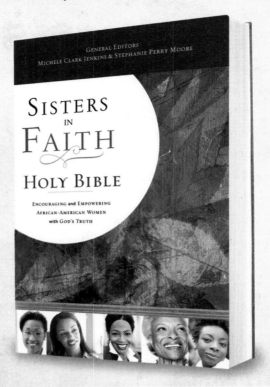

Be Filled With

God's Abundant Peace

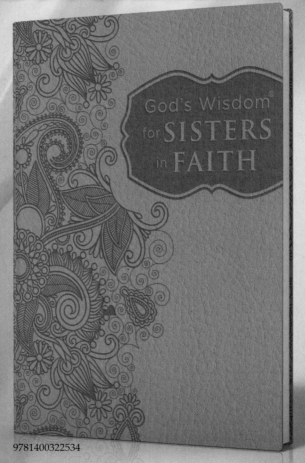

God's Wisdom® for SISTERS in FAITH

9781400322534

God's Wisdom® for Sisters in Faith brings encouragement amidst the struggles and demands of life. Featuring devotional content from the *Sisters in Faith Devotional Bible* as well as Scripture readings, this book addresses important topics all women face, such as abiding in God's love, being anxious in nothing, praying for one another, and developing strength for the journey.

AVAILABLE APRIL 2013